Turning Your Adversity Into Victory

by
Jerry Savelle

Harrison House
Tulsa, Oklahoma

Turning Your Adversity Into Victory
ISBN 0-89274-909-1
Copyright © 1994 by Jerry Savelle Ministries
P. O. Box 748
Crowley, Texas 76036

Published by Harrison House, Inc.
P. O. Box 35035
Tulsa, Oklahoma 74153

Contents

Contents

Introduction

At the close of 1992, I was honored to be one of the featured speakers at the International Believer's Convention held in Great Britain.

One evening, as Brother Kenneth Copeland was addressing the convention, suddenly the Spirit of the Lord spoke to me. The word He gave me at that time was delivered in a rhyme. It revealed what God intended to do beginning in 1993.

I received this word for myself and was so blessed by it that I shared it with those in attendance when I rose to deliver to them the message that I am presenting to you in these pages.

What the Lord spoke to my heart that evening was a specific word not only for 1993, but for future years as well. I believe this message was for all believers — for you too — if you are willing to receive it:

As you prepare to enter 1993,

You'll be walking in greater glory and greater victory.

But you must remember to keep your eyes on Me,

For it is only then that you can truly see

That the battle is not over as the enemy would say.

No, it's not over until I've had My way.

He cannot win, nor will you fail,

For I will hold back the forces of hell.

Yes, the greatest days of your life are just ahead.

So meditate on these things and don't forget what I've said.

Times of great joy and victory, too,

This is what the future holds for you.

So let Me work and don't get in My way,

And you'll see these things come to pass without delay.

Then He ended His remarks to me — and to you — with this phrase:

Every setback you've experienced in '92 will be turned into triumph by the time I am through!

You and I serve a God today Who is capable of turning every setback into a triumph, every stumbling block into a stepping stone, every curse into a blessing. That is the basic message I want to share with you in this book. May God open your heart to receive that word as from the Lord.

1

The Things Which Are Seen Are Subject To Change

Hope deferred maketh the heart sick....
                                    Proverbs 13:12
Heaviness in the heart of man maketh it stoop....
                                    Proverbs 12:25

Notice that in these passages the Lord reveals to us through the writer of the book of Proverbs two things that have an effect on the heart. When the Bible speaks of the heart of a person, it is not referring to the organ that pumps blood through the body, but to the spirit of that individual. So when it says that hope deferred makes the heart sick, it is saying that hope deferred makes the spirit man sick. It causes the spirit to malfunction.

The Creative Spirit

In Proverbs 20:27 we are told that the spirit of a man is the candle of the Lord. Therefore our spirit is made by God to be creative, to be productive. It is to be our spiritual production center.

In Matthew 12:35 Jesus said that out of the good treasure of a good man's heart issue forth good things. So the things that you and I desire to come to pass in our life are produced in our spirit as we program it with the Word of God.

Our spirit is like a creative computer. It will produce whatever we program into it. If we continually program

9

into our spirit negative things, evil things, bad things, undesirable things, then that is exactly what our spirit will produce. This is a spiritual law.

In the preceding verse (Matt. 12:34) Jesus also said that out of the abundance of the heart the mouth speaks. That means that whatever we put into our heart, into our spirit, will eventually issue forth from our mouth and will cause to come to pass whatever we say. That happens because our spirit is creative; it has creative force because it was made in the image and likeness of God. (Gen. 1:26,27.)

God is creative. Since we are made in His image and likeness, so are you and I.

The Negative Effects of Hopelessness

The Word of God says that hope deferred makes the heart sick, or causes your spirit to malfunction.

When our hope has been destroyed, not only is our heart made sick, not only is our spirit crushed, but our outlook is affected; our future is made to appear dismal. As a result, we become depressed, disheartened, and discouraged. When we lose hope, we lose the power to create the positive things that we want to see come to pass in our own lives and in the lives of those around us.

Many people in our society today are hopeless because of what they have been told, what they have allowed to lodge and take root in their hearts. They are without hope because of what they see with their eyes and hear with their ears. They are hopeless because of what they have experienced in the past.

As if that weren't enough, the media reports daily what is taking place all around us — and much of that is bad news. Every day that passes, we are inundated with negative reports about the economy, the political and educational systems, the social and moral climate, the national and international scene. If we subsist on a steady diet of that type of negative input, we soon become burdened, heavy of heart. It is no wonder that so many people are malfunctioning today, because their hope has been deferred and their hearts have become stooped and heavy.

But, thank God, the reports we receive through the news media are not the final word. The secular media can only report events and situations as they exist or occur; they cannot tell us what the Word of the Lord has to say about those events and situations. That is why, although we Christians continue to follow the daily news in order to keep abreast of what is happening in the world around us, we must not allow it to affect our outlook for the future. If we do so, we will end up being a people without hope. For there seems to be very little going on today outside the Church to inspire hope.

The Positive Effects of Hopefulness

As believers, we should be very positive people. Why? Because we have the Word of God, His **exceeding great and precious promises** (2 Pet. 1:4) for us and our loved ones. And the Bible assures us that in Christ all the promises of God are **yea** and **amen** (2 Cor. 1:20), which means "affirmative" and "so be it." You just can't get any more positive than that!

I am not talking about the power of positive thinking or mind over matter. Neither am I referring to mind science or metaphysics. I am talking about the power of the Living Word of God. When it explodes in our heart, it will transform us from hopeless, stooped, heavy-hearted individuals into hope-filled, positive, creative, people — which is what the children of God are supposed to be.

If the Apostle Paul were alive today, he probably would not be a member in good standing in most churches. Why not? Because he was too positive. Most religious people today would mistake his faith and his hope for egotism. They would mistake his positive outlook for arrogance. I know, because that is precisely the way some of them look at me and at anyone who dares to think and believe and speak positively in the face of all that is taking place in our society today. Yet all I do is what Paul did — I speak what I know to be the express, revealed Word and will of God.

When I say with Paul that I know in Whom I have believed, some people accuse me of being arrogant. When I say that my God shall provide all of my need according to His riches in glory by Christ Jesus, they think that's boastful and egotistical of me.

"But how do you know that?" they ask.

My answer to them is, "Because the Bible tells me so."

"Who do you think you are?" they want to know when I claim God's richest blessings as my rightful inheritance.

"The righteousness of God," I answer.

"How dare you make such an outrageous claim," they say.

And I respond, "I dare because Paul dared."

Religion does not want us to be positive, to be fully persuaded, to be secure. Religion wants us to be questioning, uncertain, insecure. That's why I am not a religious man; I'm a Christian!

A Christian is not hopeless. On the contrary, a true believer is filled with hope. And that hope is not in vain. Otherwise we would be **of all men most miserable** (1 Cor. 15:19). We are not hopeless. Because when we are hopeless, we cannot be creative, we cannot be productive, we cannot reach the goals, fulfill the purposes, and carry out the plans for which God has created, called, and commissioned us as His divine ambassadors.

The Power of Positive Expectation

God has a plan for our life. He has a purpose for us. He has victories for us to achieve. God is not the author of failure or defeat, but of victory and triumph. But in order to reach those goals, we must have great and positive expectations.

Many people will come through the prayer lines and ask me to pray for their physical healing. So I will lay hands on them and pray. A few days later I will see them in the meeting and say, "I believe that, in the name of Jesus, you are recovering." Often they will say to me, "Well, I don't really expect to get any better." That is always a shock to me. I wonder why they bothered to have me pray for them in the first place.

One man asked me to pray for his sick wife. I did so, and a couple of days later he came to me to report that she was not showing any improvement and that he didn't expect her to live.

"Well," I responded, "I wish you had told me that before we prayed, because we wasted a perfectly good prayer!"

When I pray, I expect results. What about you? Surely you don't pray for healing and then say, "Well, I asked God to heal me, but I don't expect to improve." That is hopelessness. And hope deferred makes the heart sick, which eventually affects the rest of the total person.

The Solid Rock

Some people have written negative things about the more notable ministers and evangelists of our time. One of these writers said of me in his book, "All Jerry Savelle does is go all over the United States building up people's hopes." He meant that as a criticism, but I took it as a compliment. In fact, I wrote him and thanked him for it. I said, "Yes, that is exactly what I do. I am guilty as charged."

When I get to heaven, I would much rather stand before God and be told, "Jerry Savelle, all you did was go around building up people's hopes" than to be told, "Jerry Savelle, all you did was go around deferring people's hope."

It is true that I go around building up hope, but this hope is not based on fantasy. It is firmly founded on the Word of God. That's where my hope lies. Not on what man has claimed, but on "thus saith the Lord." As the old hymn puts it, "My hope is built on nothing less than Jesus' blood and righteousness; I dare not trust the sweetest frame, but wholly lean on Jesus' name. On Christ, the Solid Rock I stand; all other ground is sinking sand, all other ground is sinking sand."[1]

Like the hymn writer, my hope is based on the Living Word of God. So should yours. Anything less than that leads to hopelessness, which ends in sickness of mind and body as well as of heart.

The World's View Versus God's View

The Bible says that every good and every perfect gift comes down from our heavenly Father in Whom there is no variableness, nor shadow of turning. (James 1:17.) And He has made it abundantly clear in His Word that He wills for His children to live in peace and health and prosperity. His divine will is the basis of our hope as believers.

This is the fundamental message I preach to everyone who will listen as I go around building up people's hope. There are those who hear the message of hope and receive it gladly, and there are those who hear it and reject it. When faced with a word from the Lord, people are confronted with a choice: receive it or reject it. There is no in-between.

---

[1]"The Solid Rock," words by Edward Mote, 1832, tune by William B. Bradbury, 1863.

Once an individual hears the word of faith which we preach, he can never again be neutral. He has to come to a place of decision: either he accepts it or he rejects it.

It is understandable why the non-believer today is hopeless. He has every right to be. But according to the Word of God, such a person is the only one entitled to hopelessness. In Ephesians 2:11,12 we are told that those who do not know God, those who are without God, those who are strangers to the covenant of promise, have no hope. But in Romans 5:1-5 the Bible tells us that ours is a God of hope and that those of us who have been justified by faith have peace with Him through the Lord Jesus Christ by Whom also we rejoice in *hope.* (v. 2.)

If you don't know God, then obviously you are entitled to be without hope. If you don't know your covenant rights, if you are not even aware that you have a covenant with God, then you have every right to be hopeless. You are expected to live by the world's standards. You are expected to be dominated and controlled by what man says rather than by what God says. Why? Because you don't know that there is any other information available to you.

Jesus said of His heavenly Father and ours: **...thy word is truth** (John 17:17). The dictionary defines the word *truth* as the highest form of reality that exists. That means that there must be a lower form of reality in existence. And the lower form of reality is what we see and hear and read in the world — what is reported daily in the media.

Now what the members of the media report to us is not a falsehood. It is not a fabrication. It is real. When they report that the economy is bad, the economy *is* bad. When they report that employment is down, employment *is* down. Statistics don't lie. What they reveal is absolutely factual; it is reality. But it is not the *ultimate* reality, the *highest form* of reality. The highest form of reality is the Word of God. And the Word of God says that the things which are seen are subject to change. (2 Cor. 4:18; Rom. 4:17.)

There is a higher form of reality than that which we experience every day in our contact with the physical realm. But the person without God, the one who is a stranger to the covenant promises, is not aware of this higher reality. Therefore all his beliefs are based entirely on what he hears from man, which he accepts as the final authority. When he hears that the economy is bad and is predicted to become even worse, he has no alternative but to accept that viewpoint as fact. Why? Because he doesn't know that there is any other source of information available to him.

/ This truth is illustrated in my own life. In the part of Louisiana where my wife Carolyn and I grew up, there was not much information available to us on this subject in those days. We were a young married couple trying to raise a family. I was in business for myself and we were doing our best just to make a living — and failing miserably at it.

Then one day Brother Kenneth Copeland came to our hometown and preached a message we had never heard before.

Now Carolyn and I were both Christians and had been raised in church. But in reality neither of us knew anything at all about the validity and integrity of the Word of God until we heard Brother Copeland speak on it night after night. We didn't know that we could take the Word of God and apply it to our daily situations. We didn't know that there was a higher form of reality available to us. Instead, we accepted without question whatever the world presented to us as truth.

If I watched television and the commercial said, "There's a big headache out there waiting for you," I got ready for it. I bought whatever product they were selling to ease the headache they had just talked me into receiving.

If the TV announcer said, "As long as there are winters and husbands, there will be the flu," I got ready to get the flu. Because I knew it was winter and I was a husband. I bought their product because I first bought their philosophy.

In the same way, if the news media reported that we were in a recession, I accepted that report as fact, and as a result my business soon reflected it.

Like everyone else we knew, we were limited to carnal knowledge, to what the world says, rather than being open to revelation knowledge, to what the Word says. Consequently, we were pretty hopeless. We accepted the reports of the media, of medical science, of the economists, of the so-called experts as final authority.

But once we heard and received the message of faith, once we came to understand that we did not have to live that way anymore, that we had a covenant agreement with Almighty God, signed and sealed in the blood of Jesus Who is its Guarantee and Surety, then our whole lives were revolutionized. Not only did we have hope and faith, our spirit man could finally begin to be creative and to produce the way God intended and designed it. ✓

We were no longer restricted, confined, and limited. In fact, we had unlimited potential.

That is the message that I am sharing with you in these pages. That is the discovery that I want you to make so that your life will be revolutionized and your situation changed — for good.

All Things Can Change

There are many sick people in our society today whose illness and disease is caused by hopelessness. I don't have exact statistical proof, but I would say that 85 percent of the patients in hospitals are there because of hopelessness.

17

Even medical science recognizes the fact that the mental and emotional state of a patient has much to do with his physical state.

Hopelessness can and does affect the mind and the body. That is no longer a subject of debate either in the medical world or in the spiritual world. And the reason so many people are hopeless is because they cannot foresee their personal situation — whatever it may be — ever turning around. They cannot foresee their physical crisis, financial crisis, family crisis, or any other kind of crisis ever getting any better.

In the pages that follow, I want to show you from the Word of God that the Lord is a Master, a Champion at turning the impossible into the possible. (Luke 18:27.) I don't know what is troubling you today, but I can tell you this: if you will not accept that symptom or circumstance or situation as final authority, then God can turn it around for you.

One of the greatest revelations I ever received came to me when I read what Paul had written in 2 Corinthians 4:18: **While we look not at the things which are seen, but at the things which are not seen: for the things which are seen are temporal; but the things which are not seen are eternal.**

When the Spirit of God defined for me what the word *temporal* means, He said it this way: "The things which are seen are subject to change." That statement absolutely released me.

The things which are seen are subject to change.

If you can ever see your situation as temporal, as not being permanent, you too will be absolutely released, totally set free.

If anything can be perceived by the five physical senses, then it is not permanent. It is subject to change. And the thing that will cause it to change is your hope, your faith, and your expectations, which are produced by the Word of God that you are inputting into your spirit on a daily basis.

There Is Always Hope

So although it is understandable that those people who are without God and strangers to the covenant of promise are without hope, it is not understandable for believers to be that way. In fact, it is unnatural for a believer to be hopeless. The two words *believer* and *hopeless* do not go together; they are opposites. A "hopeless believer" is a contradiction in terms. It is a violation of spiritual law.

How can anyone be a believer and be hopeless? He can't. Belief and hopeless are mutually exclusive. Belief negates hopeless, and vice versa.

Yet there are many, many hopeless Christians today. As a matter of fact, the world is full of them. What's even worse, churches are filled with them. And that is an unnatural situation. It's like seeing a fish trying to swim down the middle of main street. A fish on land is out of his natural habitat. So is a Christian who is wallowing in despair and hopelessness.

It is not natural for a person to go to church, carry a Bible, speak in tongues, listen to cassette-taped faith messages, read spiritual books, stay tuned to Christian radio, and watch Christian TV, and still be hopeless. Yet all too often in our nation today, that seems to be the case.

In our country there are literally millions of faith-filled cassette tapes being bought every year. Religious tape production is a billion-dollar industry. In fact, many Christians won't even buy a car unless it has a tape player. They will do without an air-conditioner or even a heater before they will give up their automobile tape deck.

The sale of Bibles and paperback religious books is at an all-time high. Millions are purchased all over this land every year. There is hardly a room in any of our homes that does not contain at least one Bible or spiritual book.

In America, the radio dial and the television screen are covered with Christian broadcasts twenty-four hours a day, seven days a week.

The size of the mailing lists of ministries and churches has reached phenomenal proportions. Each month we receive newsletters from preachers all over the country. And it seems that every one of them contains seven steps to this, six steps to that, and five steps to get the other steps straight.

Gospel campmeetings abound in every city. I preach in churches all over this nation, and I cannot possibly accept the invitations to all the campmeetings to which I'm invited everywhere I go. There are dozens of them, and most of them last at least a week.

Our churches are bulging at the seams with three and four services on Sunday and many others during the week.

With that flood of spiritual information, instruction, and direction at our disposal, why would any believer in his right mind ever be hopeless? It is unnatural. It is unnecessary. It is also dangerous. Our spirit man was not designed by God to function under that load of oppression and heaviness.

But, thank God, we can be delivered from it.

2
The Role of Hope
in the Life of the Believer

Hope deferred maketh the heart sick: but when the desire cometh, it is a tree of life.

Proverbs 13:12

Heaviness in the heart of man maketh it stoop: but a good word maketh it glad.

Proverbs 12:25

Here in the second part of these verses is the remedy for the heart that is stooped and heavy because of deferred hope. Besides the actual coming of the desire, the best remedy for heaviness of heart is a good word.

If you are oppressed, if there is heaviness in your heart, then the way to get delivered from that oppression is not only to see your desire realized, but also to hear a good word regarding that desire.

If you are having trouble overcoming your depression and despair, maybe it is because you have been looking to the wrong source and listening to the wrong information. Maybe you have been dwelling on, meditating on, focusing on, things that produce hopelessness rather than happiness. Maybe you need to change your source of information and start looking for a good word that will make you glad instead of sad.

The Blessings of a Merry Heart

A merry heart doeth good like a medicine: but a broken spirit drieth the bones.

Proverbs 17:22

The Bible says that a merry heart is better than a heavy heart because while a heavy heart brings sickness, a merry heart acts like a medicine.

That's what this book is all about, the blessing that comes from having a merry heart rather than a heavy heart. The difference is in the word or message on which the heart is allowed to dwell.

I assure you that not one word in this entire book will present anything to you but a good word, one that will do your heart good like a medicine. One that will cause your spirit to soar, your faith to be energized, and your hope and your expectations to rise to new heights.

Once you have grasped this concept of the importance of a merry heart, don't allow anyone to take it from you, no matter how famous or renowned he may be. Don't let anyone — regardless of how sincere or well-intended — to talk you out of your hope, your faith, your positive expectation.

It is sad to say, but some of the best-known media preachers in America, some of the most revered theologians of our time, try to talk us out of this every day. But those of us who believe in this message of faith and hope won't allow it. Do you know why? Because we know that this message works.

There is a popular saying, "If it ain't broke, don't fix it." That is the philosophy we follow. We know that what we are preaching works, so we don't try to change it. Nor do we allow anyone else to do so.

That does not mean that we don't have to face hardship and adversity, that we don't have to repel attacks against us, that we don't have to overcome obstacles or triumph over opposition. The fact is that we preachers of faith and hope get knocked down just like everyone else. But, thank God, when that happens, we pick ourselves up, brush ourselves off, and start all over again.

I am not going to stop preaching and practicing this message. Why? Because I know it works. A good word *does* make the heart glad, and a merry heart *is* like a medicine. That's why I keep delivering that good word, why I keep "going around building up people's hopes," and why I will continue to do so as long as I have breath in me. I do that because I believe it is my divine calling.

Called To Speak a Word in Season

The Lord God hath given me the tongue of the learned, that I should know how to speak a word in season to him that is weary....

Isaiah 50:4

This speaking the good word is not just an Old Testament teaching and practice. In *The New International Version* the author of Hebrews 10:25 writes: **...let us encourage one another....**

Encouragers, edifiers, that is what you and I ought to be to one another. We should be Joshuas and Calebs to one another, those who speak good words to one another so that our spirits can continually soar in the Lord.

Some of us are called "preachers." A better word would be "exhorters," those who, like Isaiah, are called to speak "a word in season to him that is weary."

But how can I do that if I myself am oppressed, hopeless, and weary? That's the problem with many preachers today: they preach their experiences rather than the Word of God. And the sad thing is that there are always those who will go to listen to that kind of message instead of giving heed to the good word that gladdens the heart.

I know what it is like to be oppressed, and I know what it is like to be delivered from that oppression. That's why I can preach this message with such enthusiasm and conviction. Because I've been on both sides of the issue. I know what it's like to be hopeless, and I know what it's like to have great hope. I know what it's like to be weary, and I also know what it's like to be refreshed. I know what it's like to be heavy-hearted, stooped, and oppressed, and, praise God, I also know what it's like to soar in the spirit and to have great expectations.

The writer of Proverbs tells us that a good word will make our heart glad. If we do not have a glad heart, then it is obvious that we need to change our source of information. We need a new outlook, a new attitude, and a new viewpoint. We need to be like the Apostle Paul who knew how to look at every situation of life — whether good or bad — and to draw from it a positive reinforcement.

Crisis or Opportunity?

But I would ye should understand, brethren, that the things which happened unto me have fallen out rather unto the furtherance of the gospel.
Philippians 1:12

As we look at the life of Paul, we see the important role that hope plays in the life of the believer. Even the greatest crisis of his life was transformed into a time of great encouragement because of his attitude. Despite the way things looked, Paul would not allow himself to become discouraged. As a result, the Lord was able to take a major setback and transform it into a major victory.

Remember that Paul was writing this letter to a church that was very intimate with his ministry. This was a partner church. In Philippians 4:15, Paul noted that this was one of the few churches that communicated with him concerning giving and receiving. These people supported his ministry. They believed in him, as they had done from the very beginning up until this time in which he was placed in bonds for preaching the Gospel.

These people knew that Paul was in prison and was facing death. They realized the seriousness of his situation.

They understood the reason he was writing them this letter. First of all, they had sent one of the members of their congregation to Paul with an offering. When he arrived, the messenger became ill and Paul ministered to him, restored him, and sent him back with this letter for the church. Paul wanted to thank them for remembering him again with their contribution. And he wanted to encourage them to continue in faith, to keep their eyes on God and their thoughts on things that were pure and holy.

As we read in Philippians 4, we see that he also wanted to remind them that because of their liberal giving and their partnership with him, his God was going to supply all of their needs according to His riches in glory by Christ Jesus. (Phil. 4:19.)

Yet, though Paul was in prison and facing death when he wrote this letter, he did not spend time magnifying his problem.

Wouldn't it be nice if we could receive more letters from preachers who are going through crisis situations yet who magnify the answer rather than the problem? I don't know about you, but I get tired of receiving those kinds of negative letters. In fact, I read the outside of the envelope to determine whether or not I'm going to open it. If the envelope is written in the sender's blood or if it is marked "Urgent, please open quickly, we're dying," then I don't even open it. I know already what the letter itself is going to be like. It is going to magnify the problem. And that is not what we are to do.

Paul did not magnify the problem, though he certainly had one. In fact, he probably would not even have mentioned it had it not been for what he said in verse 12, that he would not have his readers to be ignorant of what had happened to him or what it really meant.

Paul understood that these people only knew what they could see on the surface. They knew that he was in prison and facing death. But he wanted them to see beyond that.

He was saying to them, "There are some things happening here that you are not aware of. All you see is the negative. But I don't want you to make a final judgment based on what you see or have heard. Because if you do that, you will get the wrong impression and draw the wrong conclusion of what is really taking place in this situation."

Paul was aware that these people probably thought that this whole affair was destined to end in a great tragedy. That's why he wrote to inform them that although his situation may look bad on the outside, in truth it was working out for good because it was causing the further-ance of the Gospel.

Now, of course, Paul's enemies did not put him in prison in order to further the Gospel. Just the opposite. They threw him in prison to shut him up. We know that Satan was ultimately behind this plan. He wanted to silence this man of God. He could not afford to have him going about preaching such revelations. Everywhere that Paul went, revival broke out. People became stirred up. Paul's ministry was dangerous to Satan's operation. That's why he managed to have him cast into prison, there to await death and destruction.

The devil thought that by having Paul imprisoned, he could stop the spread of the Gospel. But it didn't work that way. God turned Paul's prison into a pulpit.

What does that say to you and me today? It says that our God can turn our crisis into victory.

Attitude Determines Outcome

It is important to remember that your attitude can be your best friend or your worst enemy.

Do you remember the story of David and Goliath? David's father sent him to find his brothers who were part of the army of Israel facing the Philistines. When David reached them, he was totally shocked at what he found. All the Israelites were in fear. They were hiding from one man, the champion of the Philistine army, Goliath. When David saw this, he could not believe his eyes. It was incomprehensible to him that the entire army of Israel had become fearful of this one man. That's why he said to them, **...who is this uncircumcised Philistine, that he should defy the armies of the living God?** (1 Sam. 17:26).

What David was saying is: "Who is this man? Who does he think he is? Why, he is not even circumcised."

Now what did that have to do with anything?

Circumcision was the token of the covenant between God and His people. David was saying, "This man has no covenant with God, so why should we be afraid of him?"

That is a very good point.

What was causing the men of Israel to cower down in fear? They were afraid of Goliath because he was a giant. When the Philistine army sent Goliath out to the side of that mountain to taunt and curse them, it struck fear in the heart of every soldier in the army of God — including Saul, the king. And Saul was the one about whom all the songs and ballads had been written. He was a mighty man of war, a great man of valor. Yet even he was intimidated by the appearance of this giant.

But David, who was just a boy, was not at all afraid of Goliath. What was the difference between David and the rest of the men of Israel? It was his attitude.

When the armies of Israel looked upon Goliath, all they could see was his enormous size. Their attitude and perspective was, "He's too big to kill." When David viewed Goliath, his attitude and perspective was, "He's too big to miss."

Same giant, different perspective, different attitude.

Isn't it amazing that two people with the same problem can have different attitudes about their situation? As a result, one will overcome the problem, while the other will be destroyed by it. Both have the same potential. But one has adopted the philosophy, "If it's the will of God that I be delivered, He will deliver me." The other says, "It is God's will that I be delivered, so I will stand against this problem until it is overcome."

God is not going to deliver anyone automatically. Walking around with our lip dragging the ground is not going to solve anything. Someone says, "Good morning" to us, and we answer, "It ain't over yet!" God cannot do anything for us as long as we have that kind of outlook. Even though it is His will that we succeed, we will miss out on His best for us if we have a negative attitude.

Remember what Paul said while in prison. He wrote that although everything looked bad for the moment, he knew that it was all working out for the best. He knew that there was more going on than what met the eye. That is the attitude you and I must have if we are to win the victory in our life.

Right now as I am ministering the Word of God to you in these pages, there is something going on behind the scenes that you can't see. God is working for you. The angels of the Lord are busy on your behalf. This very moment, the Holy Ghost is moving in a way that you cannot perceive with your natural eyes.

I don't know what kind of situation you are facing right now, but I do know this: you must not make your final judgment based on what you see or hear or feel. Paul told the people of his day, "Don't be misled. These things that have happened to me, as bad as they may appear in the natural, have turned out for good." What he was saying was, "You may have thought that my ministry was over, but God has decided to turn this prison into a pulpit, and

28

the Gospel is not suffering because of my being confined here. On the contrary, it is being furthered as a result of my incarceration."

It sounds to me that Satan's plan to destroy Paul and his effectiveness backfired. And I believe that will be the case for you too, if you will allow the Lord to work on your behalf just as He did for Paul in his situation. But in order for that to happen, like Paul, you must maintain a good attitude.

God Works All Things for Good

So that my bonds in Christ are manifest in all the palace, and in all other places;

And many of the brethren in the Lord, waxing confident by my bonds, are much more bold to speak the word without fear.

Philippians 1:13

Notice what Paul says in this passage. He states that his bonds have encouraged others who had been previously intimidated by the threats of the Roman government. These people had seen the bondage of Paul, and instead of being further intimidated, had actually been given confidence to share the Gospel more boldly and more effectively.

Now obviously that was not the plan of Satan. He did not intend for Paul or for others to "wax bold." His plan was not for Paul to keep preaching the Gospel even in prison and to stir up others to do the same inside the palace and outside. His plan was to so oppress and depress Paul that he would shut up, sit down in a corner, and wait to die.

Instead, Paul went right on preaching in prison, and as a result the other inmates became stirred up to do the same. Paul was saying to his Philippian followers that God had taken his jail cell and had transformed it into a revival center.

For years I had heard Christians say that what the devil intends for evil God will turn for good. That seemed to me

29

to be just a Pentecostal cliche, because although lots of people said it, very few of them seemed to believe it. I would hear them quote Romans 8:28: **And we know that all things work together for good to them that love God, to them who are the called according to his purpose.** But yet these same people never seemed to show any sign that God was working out anything for good in their lives. As far as I could tell, their testimony was all words; there was no substance to it. I saw no real evidence in their lives that God takes bad situations and works them for good for those who love Him.

Yet that is precisely what the Apostle Paul is saying in this letter to the Philippians. He is telling them that in his situation the Lord has taken what the devil meant for evil and has turned it for good — for all concerned. The good news is that what God did for Paul and the people of his day, He will do for you and me today.

Notwithstanding, Christ Is Preached

Some indeed preach Christ even of envy and strife; and some also of good will:

The one preach Christ of contention, not sincerely, supposing to add affliction to my bonds:

But the other of love, knowing that I am set for the defence of the gospel.

What then? notwithstanding, every way, whether in pretence, or in truth, Christ is preached; and I therefore do rejoice, yea, and will rejoice.

Philippians 1:15-18

Here Paul is telling the Philippians that not everyone in prison with him is preaching the Gospel for the right motive. Some are preaching out of envy, strife, and contention, thinking that by doing so they are hurting Paul.

But notice Paul's attitude. He did not care what their true motive was as long as Christ was preached. If Paul had

had the wrong attitude, he would have spent the rest of his life trying to straighten out other people, all those who were acting for the wrong reason. But he didn't do that. Instead, he rejoiced that whatever the motivation, Christ was being preached. And his attitude was contagious. It was infectious.

As followers of Jesus, as His representatives on earth, as ambassadors for Christ, you and I are supposed to be carriers of hope, carriers of faith.

Every time we walk into a hopeless situation, our very presence ought to change the atmosphere around us.

I have been in a room when Oral Roberts walked in, and everyone there would sense his presence. When he enters, something comes in with him. There is an air about him that is sensed by everyone present. Although I have never met Billy Graham personally, I have been told that the same is true of him. When he enters a room, a hush falls on the place because everyone in attendance recognizes a holy presence in their midst.

That is the way it ought to be with each and every one of us. The anointing of the Lord should be so strong on us that wherever we go, people sense it.

That has happened to me on occasion, and I am looking for it to happen more and more. One time I walked into a convenience store to buy a carton of milk. A man who was standing there reading a pornographic magazine suddenly looked at me and asked, "Who are you?"

"Pardon me?" I asked.

"Who are you?" he repeated. "You scare me."

I glanced at what he was reading and replied, "I am a minister of the Gospel, and I have been sent by God to deliver you."

Like Paul, whatever our situation in life, no matter how bad it may appear for the moment, God can and will take it and turn it for good. He will transform our prisons into revival centers so that, notwithstanding, the Gospel of Christ is preached everywhere as a witness to all people. And, like Paul, despite our personal circumstances, we will rejoice.

Victory in Life or Death

For I know that this shall turn to my salvation through your prayer, and the supply of the Spirit of Jesus Christ,

According to my earnest expectation and my hope, that in nothing I shall be ashamed, but that with all boldness, as always, so now also Christ shall be magnified in my body, whether it be by life, or by death.

For to me to live is Christ, and to die is gain.
Philippians 1:19-21

Despite his less than ideal situation, Paul is confident, assured, joyful. The reason he can be full of confidence, assurance, and joy in the face of such peril is because he knows that whatever happens to him will be for his good. Even though he is in prison and facing possible death, he is not ashamed nor afraid nor intimidated.

What can anyone do to such a man? They can't silence him, even by shutting him up in a dungeon. If they threaten to kill him, he simply says, "Go ahead, you will be doing me a favor." That's what Paul means when he says that to live is Christ, but to die is gain. That is a no-lose situation. Either way, Paul comes out a winner.

According to Your Hope and Expectation Be It Unto You

Paul writes his followers and supporters and says to them that he knows that this situation will turn to his salvation, or his deliverance.

Notice that Paul didn't write, "Please *pray* that this situation will turn out for good." Instead, he says, "I *know* it will turn out for good." Notice also what he attributes this turning to, the basis of his belief that everything will work out for the best for all concerned: "For I know that this shall turn to my salvation *through your prayer*, and *the supply of the Spirit of Jesus Christ.*" (v. 19.)

What does that mean to you and me today? It means that whatever we are facing in our lives; regardless of how severe the test, trial, or tribulation; no matter how impossible things may appear at the moment; if we have confidence in prayer and the supply of the Holy Ghost, that situation can and will turn. Any situation, no matter how dark and drear and dire it may seem, can turn for our good — if we know how to tap into the power of the Holy Spirit.

What are you going through today? Do you know how to tap into the power of the Holy Ghost? If so, then that situation will turn.

"But, brother, you don't know how terrible my situation is."

That's not the issue. The issue is, do you have a revelation of the power of prayer and the power of the Holy Ghost? If you do, then it matters not how severe the test or trial, you can see it through, you can see it turned to your advantage.

But notice also what Paul says in the next verse: "According to my earnest expectation and my hope." (v. 20.) This phrase "according to" means "in proportion to." Paul says that his situation will turn in direct proportion to his earnest expectation and his hope.

What does that say to you and me in our desperate situations of life? It says that our deliverance is based entirely on *our* expectation and *our* hope.

What do you expect God to do in your situation, whatever it may be?

"Well, brother, although we prayed together, I don't expect my wife to get any better."

Then she won't.

"Oh, I know prayer is powerful, but I really don't expect to get a job."

Then you won't.

"I appreciate your prayers, brother, but I don't expect to be healed."

Then you won't be.

"My wife and I have prayed and prayed, but I just don't expect my kids to be delivered from drugs and alcohol and sexual promiscuity."

Then they won't be.

"Are you telling me, brother, that all I have to do is say that I expect God to do this and that, and He will do it?"

No, it goes deeper than that. Expectation and hope depend upon more than just words; they depend upon a divine revelation. Once the Word of God becomes a personal revelation to you, then you will have no problem saying what you expect and giving voice to your hope. Like Paul in his situation, you will declare boldly what you expect and hope to take place — even though the masses may misunderstand and even disagree.

If you begin to speak forth your positive expectation and hope, you will stand out in a crowd. Why? Because you will be one in a million. The masses of people today don't have that kind of positive expectation, that kind of solid hope, that kind of confident assurance.

You must remember that many people in our society today are without God. They are strangers to the covenant of promise. Therefore they are without hope, without expectation. But you are not. Therefore you can boldly declare with the Apostle Paul, "I *know* that this will turn."

"But how can you know?"

Because I know how to tap into the power of prayer and the power of the Holy Ghost.

How do you *know* that your situation is going to turn? Because your hope and expectation are high. You don't tarry, you tap. You don't wait to see, you watch to see. When you pray, you expect. And what you expect comes to pass. Like Paul, you know that your situation will turn, because of your prayer and because of the supply of the spirit of Jesus Christ according to your earnest expectation and hope.

Today's Situations and Setbacks Are Tomorrow's Triumphs and Testimonies

The word from the Lord I delivered, which I discussed earlier in the book, "Every setback you've experienced in '92 will be turned into triumph by the time I am through," gives us a promise from God that is for today, not just '92. (Psalm 34:19 says: **Many are the afflictions of the righteous: but the Lord delivereth him out of them all.**)

Now I don't know what that word from the Lord does for you, but I know what it does for me: it gives me great hope, great expectation. I am expecting every setback I have experienced in the past to be turned into a triumph before God has finished.

I am not going to have the Spirit of God speak that word to my spirit and then go on with my life dwelling on my setbacks. Setbacks are temporal; therefore they are subject to change. Setbacks are nothing more than stepping stones to greater victories. God can take every setback in life and turn it into an advantage.

If you are in bondage today, remember that God can take your bondage and transform it into freedom, just as He did for Paul. God can take the very thing that Satan is using to try to shut you up, and change it into something that will give you a greater platform from which to declare the Gospel and glory of the Lord.

Satan intended to shut up Paul in prison, but God took that situation and turned it into a great platform. Paul's imprisonment didn't stop the spread of the Gospel, it caused it to spread farther than ever. Even though Paul was confined to a jail cell, he wrote the book of Philippians. Had Satan known the impact that this little book would have on future generations throughout the ages, he would never have thrown Paul into prison.

Remember, the Bible says that had the princes of this world known, they would not have crucified the Lord of glory. (1 Cor. 2:7,8.)

I like to paraphrase that passage this way: "Had the devil known, he would not have..."

Had Satan known how God was going to turn my situation, he would never have put me into that situation.

Do you know what I have learned to do? Every time the devil launches an attack against me, I tell him, "Okay, go right ahead. I just want to point out that you started this, I didn't. You ought to know better by now. You've been launching attacks like this against me and my family and ministry for more than twenty-five years, and God has always been faithful to deliver us every time.

"I want to remind you, devil, that every time you have attacked me or mine, God has turned that attack into a victory. Then I went out and preached that victory and blessed many other people. I just want you to know, Satan, that this is going to be another preaching story!"

What am I saying? I am saying that what you're going through today will be a testimony tomorrow. Therefore, make the most of it.

Confront the devil head on and tell him, "Satan, I stand against you. I have a covenant with God through the precious blood of Jesus Christ, and therefore there is no way that I can be defeated. Defeat is not in my vocabulary. No, I'm not defeated, I'm determined. I am not the victim, I am the victor. I can do all things through Christ Who strengthens me. The Spirit of the Living God indwells my being, and greater is He Who is in me than he who is in the world.

"Satan, you started this, but I'm going to finish it. When you attacked me with this problem, you just provided me another opportunity for victory. I intend to meet the challenge with the Word of God, with faith, hope, prayer, expectation, and the power of the Holy Ghost. I intend to win. And when all is said and done, when the dust has settled, I will be the victor, for my God is working right now to turn this crisis into triumph.

"I am not hopeless. On the contrary, I have great expectations. And in the end, I *will* see my desires on my enemy!" (Ps. 92:11.)

3
Attitude Brings Deliverance

What then? notwithstanding, every way, whether in pretence, or in truth, Christ is preached; and I therefore do rejoice, yea, and will rejoice.

Philippians 1:18

Thus far we have seen from the writings of the Apostle Paul and from the example of his life that this man expected God to turn every negative situation into a positive situation. He fully expected every crisis to be transformed into a triumph.

Although locked up in prison, he writes to the church in Philippi, encouraging them to take heart and not to be misled by appearances. He explains to them that, despite the way his situation may be viewed from their distant perspective, he fully expects it to turn out for good.

In verse 18 he says, in essence, "I intend to rejoice over what is happening here and to continue to rejoice." In that admittedly less than perfect circumstance, Paul was already planning what was going to take place in the future. He had already determined that, come what may in the physical realm, he was going to rejoice in the Lord.

A paraphrased translation of verse 19 reads: ...I will **keep on celebrating because I know this attitude will bring my deliverance....**[1]

---

[1]Ben Campbell Johnson, *The Heart of Paul: A Relational Paraphrase of the New Testament* (Toccoa, GA: A Great Love, Inc., Publisher, 1976), p. 138.

A Positive Attitude Produces
Positive Results

Notice Paul's attitude. It was one that Satan could not overcome, one that the Roman government could not prevail against.

Paul's attitude was very positive. Does that mean that he was what we would call today a "positive thinker"? No, Paul's confidence was not in his own thoughts, his mental capacity, his intellectual capability, or even his optimistic outlook, all of which were doubtlessly considerable. No, it was Paul's ultimate confidence in the ability of His God to turn things around that gave him such a positive expectation.

As I have noted, this is not a matter of mental gymnastics or mind over matter. What we are talking about here is not the power of positive thinking, but the power of revelation knowledge based on the Word of God. When that knowledge explodes in a person's heart, it has a profound effect on his outlook and attitude. Revelation knowledge has a keen ability to make an individual very active and energetic. Once something is revealed to a person by the Lord, that individual can no longer remain doubtful, ambivalent, or passive about that subject.

When you discover, by revelation, that you have a right to live in divine health, you won't remain doubtful, ambivalent, or passive where sickness is concerned. You will attack it with the revelation that you have received.

Revelation knowledge energizes you. It wakes you up. It enlightens and inspires you. It causes you to realize that you've been lied to by the devil, that you've been misled by many sincere Christians, that you've been deceived by religion. That realization makes you angry and aggressive so that you begin taking, by force if necessary, what you know to be rightfully yours.

Notice that Paul says that he will keep on rejoicing, keep on celebrating, because he knows that this attitude will result in his deliverance.

Your attitude is important. As we have noted, your attitude can be your best friend or your worst enemy.

Do you wake up in the morning with a bad attitude? What if somehow Psalm 118:24 became revelation knowledge to you: **This is the day which the Lord hath made; we will rejoice and be glad in it?** How would you then react to each new day, regardless of how it may appear or how you may feel when facing it? Would you be inclined to greet each dawn with an attitude of lassitude or an attitude of gratitude? Would you rise up each morning proclaiming, "This is the day the Lord has made; I will rejoice and be glad in it"?

"But, brother, I can't say that until I see out how the day is going to turn out."

No, that's backwards. That's like saying to the fireplace, "Give me some heat, and I'll throw in some wood."

To wait until you see how the day is going to go before expressing gratitude and praise to God for that day is putting the cart before the horse.

It will be a great day if you will start out with the attitude that according to the Word of God every day is a great day, and this one will be no exception, that whatever it may bring in the natural you will rejoice and be glad in it.

That is the attitude that Paul displays here in the midst of his bondage and imprisonment. He declares that he will keep on celebrating and rejoicing — despite his current situation — because he is convinced that it is his attitude that will bring his deliverance.

For I Know...

For I *know* that this shall turn to my salvation through your prayer, and the supply of the Spirit of Jesus Christ.

Philippians 1:19

As we have seen, Paul was absolutely convinced that everything was going to turn out for the best in his situation, regardless of how it may look at the moment. He knew that he would be delivered because of the prayers of those who were interceding for him and because of the supply of the Spirit of Jesus Christ.

That reveals to us that if we have confidence, if we have a revelation of the power of prayer and how to tap into the supply of the Holy Ghost, then any situation can turn in our favor. No matter how devastating a particular set of circumstances may seem at the time, no matter how long we may have been going through a time of trial or tribulation, if we know these things, then there is hope for our final deliverance.

According to My Expectation and Hope...

According to my earnest expectation and my hope....
Philippians 1:20

We receive in direct proportion to what we expect. Jesus expressed this same idea a couple of different ways: In Matthew 8:13 He told a Roman officer, **...as thou hast believed, so be it done unto thee....** In Matthew 9:29 He said to two blind men, **...According** [in proportion] **to your faith be it unto you.**

Faith produces a very positive attitude, an attitude of expectancy.

I often hear people say things like, "Well, we're just trusting God, just living by faith, and so we don't know how things are going to turn out because you never know what God is going to do."

That's not faith. Faith knows exactly what God will do. No one can live by faith and have confidence in the Lord if he is never sure what God is going to do in any given situation.

I always know what God is going to do. God is not difficult for me to understand or predict; it's people I can't figure out. God is going to do exactly what He has said in His Word, because He is not a man that He should lie, or the son of man that He should repent. (Num. 23:19.)

I will be the first to admit that I seldom know *how* God is going to fulfill His Word. But I do know *that* He is going to fulfill it. That's faith. Faith is confidence in God's ability and in His willingness to confirm His Word **with signs following**. (Mark 16:20.)

Because I have faith, I know what God is going to do: He is going to confirm His Word in my life. I don't know how He is going to do it, nor even when He is going to do it, but I do know for certain that He is going to do it.

That's why, having done all, I stand (Eph. 6:13) — on the Word of God. Because I would be a fool to give up when God has already promised that He will keep His Word, that He will watch over it to perform it (Jer. 1:12 NIV), that it will not return to Him void or empty, but that it will accomplish that which He has sent it to accomplish. (Is. 55:11.)

"But how long do you stand?"

That's simple. I stand until I win.

"How long does it take to win?"

Until you don't have to stand anymore.

What am I saying? I am saying that when we take a stand of faith, there is no compromising, no backing off, no giving up or giving out or giving in.

"Well, that's easy for you to say, brother; you don't know what I'm going through."

How do you know that? How do you know that I am not going through exactly the same thing you are right now? I have the same problems as everyone else. The difference is that, like Paul, I have learned not to magnify the problem but to magnify the solution.

Paul went through much more than most Christians will ever have to suffer. Yet he knew how to handle problems by keeping them in proper perspective. Paul's great faith did not make him immune to problems; in fact, he probably endured more hardships and difficulties than any of us ever will, yet he came through them all because he knew that his deliverance was in accordance to his hope and expectation. That is the lesson that we must learn.

Rejoice Always
Rejoice in the Lord alway: and again I say, Rejoice.
Philippians 4:4

Faith is not pretending that there is no problem. Many believers have this misconception. They think that people of faith act as if there are no problems. I'm sure that is because we have pretenders who have left that impression.

I don't pretend not to have problems. When sickness strikes my body, I don't go around saying, "That's not pain I feel. I don't believe in pain. Pain is not real."

That's not faith, that's stupidity.

When the house rent is due, I don't say, "That's not true. I don't owe any rent. I don't believe in paying rent. I'm not going to talk to my landlord because I don't really owe him anything."

That's not faith; that's stupidity.

When my wife gets upset with me, I don't say, "I don't believe in marital disagreements. I don't have a problem with my wife; in fact, I don't even have a wife!"

That's not faith; that's stupidity.

Faith never denies the existence of a problem. Faith attacks the problem with the Word of God. Faith recognizes that although the problem is real, there is a higher reality called truth. That truth is the Word of God. When the two come into conflict, then either the problem wins, or the truth wins. And truth never fails.

That is what Paul is saying here in this letter to the church in Philippi. He is not pretending that he has no problem. He is stating that he believes his problem will be turned into victory. He is saying that he is going to go on rejoicing in the face of his problem because he knows that it is his attitude in regard to that problem that will result in his deliverance.

That's why he writes to the Philippians to rejoice. Notice that Paul says to rejoice *always*, not just when everything is going well.

Why does he write that to them and to us? Because he has learned the secret to facing every hard situation of life. He has learned not to allow anything to change his attitude. He has learned that in spite of his circumstances he must not become oppressed or depressed or hopeless or to allow heaviness to come into his spirit and choke his faith.

Instead, he has learned to keep on rejoicing, to keep on celebrating, because he knows that his attitude of gratitude will eventually bring his deliverance. It is time that we in the Body of Christ learn this lesson. We need to remember that **a merry heart doeth good like a medicine**. (Prov. 17:22.) We need to learn to laugh more. Every time we face a problem, we need to learn to smile, to release our joy. Not after the victory has been won, but while we are waiting for it.

In fact, you will find that thanksgiving and praise and the release of joy is the greatest expression of faith known to man. When you can thank God hilariously before the deliverance has come, that is truly the highest expression of faith of which anyone is capable.

Suppose someone I don't know offers to buy me a new suit of clothes. In order for me to benefit from that offer, I must do three things: First, I must assume that the person has the means to fulfill his offer. Second, I must assume that he is a man of his word, that he will do what he has said he will do. Finally, I must accept his offer, which is usually expressed in thanks. /

What would the man think if I responded to his offer by saying, "Well, that's very nice of you, I'm sure; but if you don't mind, I will save my thanks until I see the suit of clothes"? He would likely think that I needed to learn some manners. He might even conclude that I didn't deserve a new suit of clothes after all.

Yet that is precisely what we do to God all the time. We pray, "Oh, Lord, I am believing You to deliver me from this situation."

Then the Lord says to us, "Then thank Me for it."

"Oh no, Lord, as soon as I am released from this situation, then I'll praise You. I'll shout and jump and dance then, but not before, not until I have seen my deliverance."

No, that's backwards. It's ill-mannered. It's also faithless.

If God is going to make a promise to us, then first of all, He must have the resources to back up that promise. If God says that He will supply all our needs according to His riches in glory by Christ Jesus, then God evidently has riches in glory by Christ Jesus; otherwise, He has no business making such an offer.

Do you know why? Because somebody like you or me is bound to take Him up on it. We are going to act on His promise. And if He doesn't have the resources to fulfill His promise, then He is a liar. If God didn't mean to keep His promise, then He shouldn't have allowed it to be recorded in the Bible. Because there are people like you and me who don't have any better sense than to act on it.

But I have discovered over the past twenty-odd years that not only does God have the necessary resources, but that He is faithful to keep His Word.

That's why Paul could boast with such confidence, "I *know* that my attitude will bring my deliverance." He knew Who he was dealing with.

I believe that one of the major reasons so many people never experience deliverance is because they have never demonstrated this kind of attitude of gratitude while waiting for that deliverance to be manifested. They have never learned to do as Paul and to keep on rejoicing and celebrating until the deliverance is brought forth.

I Know That I Shall Live

For me to live is Christ, and to die is gain.

But if I live in the flesh, this is the fruit of my labour: yet what I shall choose I wot not.

For I am in a strait betwixt two, having a desire to depart, and to be with Christ; which is far better:

Nevertheless to abide in the flesh is more needful for you.

And having this confidence, I know that I shall abide and continue with you all for your furtherance and joy of faith.

Philippians 1:21-25

Notice that Paul has a problem here. He is endeavoring to make a decision concerning his future. He says that he is not sure whether he should live or die.

Note that he doesn't even mention the Roman government. He acts as though they have no part to play in

47

this matter. He speaks as if it is his choice entirely, not theirs.

The reason he is "in a strait betwixt two" is because he knows that for him to die would be gain, the fulfillment of his ultimate goal, since he would go on to be with the Lord Jesus. But, on the other hand, he also knows that it would be better for his followers if he lived. That's the dilemma he is facing. If he had his way, he would die and go on to heaven; but he knows that he is still needed on earth.

Then in verse 25 he solves his own dilemma. He makes his decision and states without a shadow of a doubt, "I *know* that I *shall abide* and *continue* with you all for your furtherance of joy and faith."

Let's look at verse 26 in the paraphrased translation: **...so that I may help you grow in the faith and celebrate life more fully.**[2]

In other words, what Paul is saying to the believers in Philippi is: "I know I must remain so I can teach you how to have an attitude of gratitude, even in the midst of a crisis. I want to teach you how to maintain a thankful spirit even when there seems to be nothing around you to be thankful for. I want to teach you how to rejoice when there is absolutely no natural cause for rejoicing."

Don't Let Satan Steal Your Joy

In Psalm 116:17 David wrote of the Lord, **I will offer to thee** *the sacrifice of thanksgiving....* When is the giving of thanks to the Lord a "sacrifice"? It is a sacrifice when the worshipper doesn't *feel like* giving thanks.

All of us will admit, I am sure, that there are times in our life when we do not feel like giving thanks to God. No

---

[2]Ben Campbell Johnson, *The Heart of Paul: A Relational Paraphrase of the New Testament* (Toccoa, GA: A Great Love, Inc., Publisher, 1976), p. 138.

matter who we are, there are many things that rob us of the joy of our salvation, the joy of giving thanks to the Lord. This can cause us to have a negative attitude. In fact, if we are totally honest, we will have to confess that we have to guard ourselves against negativism quite often. That is true of the best of us — even preachers of the Gospel.

Usually it is not the big things that rob us of our joy, it is the little things.

It's not waking up in the morning and having a 747 airliner drop down on our house that steals our joy in the Lord. More often it is waking up and having a "bad hair day." Some of us, I am sure, lose our joy every Sunday morning just in the process of getting ourselves and our family up and dressed and transported in one piece down to the church. How often have we lost our joy over something as minute as a lost button that popped off our suit just as we were getting into the car?

Just as it is the little foxes that spoil the vines (Song of Sol. 2:15), so it is the minor irritations and trivial inconveniences in our daily life that most often rob us of our joy. It may not sound as though it amounts to much at the moment, but over a period of time it can build up and become a serious problem. What is happening in that situation is that the devil is putting us to the test. He is pushing us to the limit of our patience and endurance to see what "ticks us off," what aggravates us to distraction, what causes us to lose control and react negatively. Once he discovers what that is, he will keep on attacking us in that area so he can keep us in a continual joyless attitude.

Why is it so important to the devil to steal our joy? Because he knows that the joy of the Lord is our strength. (Neh. 8:10.) If we don't have any joy, we don't have any strength. If we have no strength, we have no resistance. If we cannot resist the devil, he won't flee from us. If Satan doesn't flee from us, we don't win. It is a vicious cycle.

Whether you realize it or not, whether you believe it or not, Satan wants your joy. He wants your attitude of gratitude. He wants your positive expectation. He wants you getting up in the morning and instead of boldly proclaiming, "This is the day the Lord has made; I will rejoice and be glad in it!" to murmur and complain, "This is gonna be a lousy day; I can tell it already." He wants you to wake up every Monday morning dismally declaring it a "Blue Monday." He wants you to face each new day fully expecting it to be a disaster and fully expecting God to do nothing about it.

Paul knew all this. That's why he wrote to the believers in Philippi that, although he would prefer to depart and be with the Lord, he was certain that he was going to go on living so he could teach them how to grow in faith and how to celebrate life more fully.

Life is good. Life is enjoyable. Life is fun. It is exciting to be a Christian. It is invigorating to face and overcome challenges. It is satisfying and fulfilling to grow in faith. It is wonderful to be able to give thanks to God and to celebrate the life He has bestowed upon us in all its fullness and abundance.

4

God Can Turn Any Situation

Looking unto Jesus the author and finisher of our faith; who for the joy that was set before him endured the cross, despising the shame, and is set down at the right hand of the throne of God.

Hebrews 12:2

One time I asked the Lord, "How could You possibly endure Calvary and all its suffering and shame with joy? You knew You were going to be made sin. You knew You were going to be made a curse. You knew You were going to be oppressed and smitten, abused and tortured. You knew You were going to be spat upon, laughed at, mocked, scorned, and ridiculed. You knew You were going to have a crown of thorns placed on Your head, nails driven into Your hands, and a spear thrust into Your side. You knew You were going to be forsaken and die alone in anguish and pain. How could You endure all that with joy?"

He said to me, "I could endure all that with joy because I knew how it was going to turn out."

As followers and imitators of Christ, you and I can endure anything as long as we know its final outcome.

"But I don't know that!"

Then you should read the Bible. That's what it has been given to us for, to reveal to us how it is all going to turn out.

"But, brother, where does the Bible tell us that?"

For one place, in Psalm 34:19: **Many are the afflictions of the righteous: but the Lord delivereth him out of them all.**

I don't know about you, but since I am the righteous, since I have been made the righteousness of God in Christ (2 Cor. 5:21), that tells me how *my* situation is going to turn out. Therefore, whatever the circumstance I find myself facing, no matter how dismal it may appear, regardless of how difficult it may be for a time, I can endure it with joy. I can do that because all the time I am being afflicted, I am looking to Jesus, the Author and Finisher of my faith. All during my trials and tribulations, throughout my sufferings and afflictions, I am keeping my eyes on the Lord Who delivers me out of them all.

That is a lesson every Christian needs to learn.

Give Thanks Always, Triumph Always

Now thanks be unto God which always causeth us to triumph in Christ, and maketh manifest the savour of his knowledge by us in every place.
2 Corinthians 2:14

Paul incorporated into his life this attitude of gratitude, this thanksgiving, this celebrating, this rejoicing that he prescribed to others.

Notice that immediately after exhorting the Philippians to rejoice in the Lord always (Phil. 4:4), Paul also exhorted them: **Be careful** [anxious] **for nothing; but in every thing by prayer and supplication** *with thanksgiving* **let your requests be made known unto God** (Phil 4:6).

Rejoicing and thanksgiving are such an integral part of the faith life of Paul that they cannot be removed. When he prays, he rejoices and gives thanks to God. When he walks in faith, he rejoices and gives thanks to God. When things are going well, he rejoices and gives thanks to God. And when he is in adversity, he rejoices and gives thanks to God.

Obviously, somewhere along the way, the Apostle Paul learned how to celebrate life fully. Just as he counseled the Philippians, he gave thanks to God always.

Now this word *always* can be defined simply as "without exception." Regardless of his situation, whether good or bad, Paul gave thanks to God, rejoicing in the Lord, without exception. He could do that because, as he wrote to his followers in Philippi, he knew that it was his attitude in regard to any situation of life that would bring about his ultimate deliverance from that situation.

The same is true of us. That's why we need to learn to do as Paul taught, and as Paul practiced. We need to learn to rejoice *always*, and to give thanks to God *always*. Why? Because we know that, regardless of our situation, He *always* causes us to triumph.

The key word here is *causes*. That word gives the implication that our triumph may not come instantly, it may not appear overnight, but if we will continue to persevere, eventually God will cause us to be victorious.

In Psalm 37:5, David wrote: **Commit thy way unto the Lord; trust also in him; and he shall bring it to pass.** Later, in the New Testament, Paul echoed this same idea when he wrote to the Corinthians to give thanks to God Who will always cause them to triumph. (2 Cor. 2:14.) If we will trust our situation to God, whatever it may be, He will bring us through to victory. He will deliver us. He will bring it to pass. He will cause it to happen.

Sometimes we read in the Bible where God brought something to pass, or caused something to happen suddenly. Many times, however, that sudden event occurred only after a long period of waiting and watching. In the book of Hebrews we are exhorted to be followers of those who through *faith* and *patience* inherit the promises of God. (Heb. 6:12.) God's promised triumph does not always come quickly or easily. It is the result of faith and patience and perseverance.

That's why we must never give up, never write off anything as a bad experience or a lost cause. We must stay with it until God turns it around and causes us to triumph. But He cannot do that if we are not willing to stand, and having *done all*, to stand. We cannot expect to triumph in any given situation of life if we are not willing to see that situation through to eventual victory — regardless of how long it may take.

In Galatians 6:9, Paul echoes these same words as in the book of Hebrews and his message of encouragement to the Philippians when he writes: **And let us not be weary in well doing: for in due season we shall reap, if we faint not.** The man who wrote these words was not a novice. He was a seasoned veteran. This was a man who had seen it all, who had been through it all. When he says that God will always cause us to triumph, he knows what he is talking about.

In the mind of God, no situation is hopeless, no one is beyond redemption or deliverance, there is no end but triumph. What we must ask ourselves is, how desperately do we want that triumph? If we want it so much that we will stand, and having done all to stand, then God will grant us that victory, as we see in His Word.

Why Sit We Here?

> ...there were four leprous men at the entering in of the gate: and they said one to another, Why sit we here until we die?
>
> If we say, We will enter into the city, then the famine is in the city, and we shall die there: and if we sit still here, we die also. Now therefore come, and let us fall unto the host of the Syrians: if they save us alive, we shall live; and if they kill us, we shall but die.
>
> **2 Kings 7:3,4**

You are probably familiar with this story from the Old Testament. It concerns four lepers who were the least likely to succeed of anybody I have ever read about.

The reason they were such unlikely candidates for success is because they had three strikes against them. Number one, they suffered from leprosy. They knew full well that at some point this dreaded disease was going to kill them. Number two, they were starving to death. Enemy forces had come in and surrounded their city, cutting off its supply lines and causing a famine in the area. Not even the rich could buy food because there was none to be had. And because of their disease, these poor men were not even allowed into the city gates to beg for whatever food there might have been. Number three, the enemy was about to attack and destroy everyone. Like so many vultures, they were just waiting until the inhabitants of that city had become weak and unable to resist.

So these four men did not face a very promising future. If their leprosy didn't kill them, then they would die of starvation — if the enemy didn't come and put them to the sword first. If anyone had a right to have a bad attitude, it was these guys. In the natural, they had nothing to live for, nothing to hope for, nothing to motivate them, to inspire and encourage them.

And you and I think we have problems. Now I am not belittling or demeaning your situation, but surely it can't be as desperate, as devastating, as the situation in which these poor fellows found themselves. But, as we will see, something happened to change their situation. And it happened when they had a change of attitude.

"Why sit we here until we die?" they asked themselves.

That question was tremendously important. It eventually brought about a change not only in these men's supposedly hopeless situation, but in the situation of many others who seemed to be as destined for death and destruction as they were.

The reason that question changed these men's situation is because it changed their response to their situation.

Instead of sitting and waiting to die, they decided to do something, to take action. Their attitude was, "If death is coming for us, then it is going to have to get us on the move because we are not going to just sit here and passively wait for it. We are going to get up and go to the camp of the enemy. If they let us live, fine. If they kill us, at least we will have made an effort."

So they went into action. Instead of sitting there in misery and despair, instead of feeling sorry for themselves, instead of moaning and complaining and crying, "Woe is us; there is no hope, no way out," they stood to their feet and set themselves into motion.

Many Christians today are sitting in utter defeat without ever having even risen to their feet and entered the battle. That is so tragic, and so unnecessary.

Remember, the battleground is in the mind. The battle is waged while we are sitting at the table, or driving through town, going about our daily routine. It is there that the victory or the defeat is determined. All the time we are accepting defeat, God is saying to us, "I will cause you to triumph." That's why we need to learn a lesson from these four lepers and decide to do something about our situation before it is too late.

Why sit we here until we die?

They Rose Up

And they rose up in the twilight, to go unto the camp of the Syrians: and when they were come to the uttermost part of the camp of Syria, behold, there was no man there.

For the Lord had made the host of the Syrians to hear a noise of chariots, and a noise of horses, even the noise of a great host: and they said one to another, Lo, the king of Israel hath hired against us the kings of the Hittites, and the kings of the Egyptians, to come upon us.

Wherefore they arose and fled in the twilight, and left their tents, and their horses, and their asses, even the camp as it was, and fled for their life.

And when these lepers came to the uttermost part of the camp, they went into one tent, and did eat and drink, and carried thence silver, and gold, and raiment, and went and hid it; and came again, and entered into another tent, and carried thence also, and went and hid it.

Then they said to one another, We do not well: this day is a day of good tidings, and we hold our peace: if we tarry till the morning light, some mischief will come upon us: now therefore come, that we may go and tell the king's household.

2 Kings 7:5-9

So these men arose. They got up and went into action.

I am convinced that as soon as these four lepers began to walk toward the enemy's camp, the Lord caused their footsteps to be magnified so that they sounded like the marching tread of a mighty army. That's what the Syrians heard as they sat in their camp with plenty to eat and drink, waiting for the people of Israel to die of starvation and deprivation. They heard the sound of chariots and horses and thousands of disciplined troops. As a result, they were so frightened, they did not even send out a scout to see how large the approaching army was. Instead, they leaped to their feet and fled in utter terror, leaving behind all their food and drink, all their gold and silver, all their clothing and weapons of war.

Here was a no-win situation that God turned into a triumph. I believe that God is ready to do the same in our situation. All He is waiting for is for us to get up, brush ourselves off, and to boldly declare, "Satan, I am not sitting here until I die! I am not going to accept defeat! I am going to go into action! And I will be victorious!"

Notice the irony of this situation: the mighty army of the Syrians did just what the four poor Israeli lepers refused to do; they gave up without a fight. As a result, they lost everything. And the lepers won everything. The battle was decided in the mind of these four "hopeless" outcasts. The first step to victory is a changed attitude.

God hasn't forgotten how to fool the enemy. The devil bought that trick, and he will buy God's next one too. I have sometimes joked about buying a cassette tape with the sound of marching feet on it and playing it for the devil every once in a while. I would say to him, "There's an army coming, boy. You'd better get outta here." But, of course, that is not what runs the devil off; it is the Word of God that causes him to flee.

Satan cannot stand what Oral Roberts has called the "march of faith." He hates it. It is time for the Body of Christ to rise up, fall into formation, and begin to march forward to drive the enemy from our God-given territory. It is time for us to draw our swords, dust them off, sharpen them to a razor edge, and lay on the attack. I can assure you that if we will do so, the devil and all his demonic hordes will flee, just as the Syrians fled in stark terror at the sound of the marching army of the Lord.

What does this story of the four lepers say to us today? It says that in the mind of God it is triumph, not defeat, that is inevitable in our lives — *if* we will have the courage to rise up and step forth in the march of faith.

Curses Turned to Blessings

Nevertheless the Lord thy God would not hearken unto Balaam; but the Lord thy God *turned* the curse into a blessing unto thee, because the Lord thy God loved thee.

Deuteronomy 23:5

In the following pages, I would like to quote several verses that contain the word *turn* or *turned.* I do that in an effort to impress upon you the fact that God can turn your situation around, that He can turn your curses into blessings, just as He did for the children of Israel in Old Testament days.

God can turn your financial crisis into the greatest financial miracle you have ever experienced in your life. He can turn your sickness, even your "incurable" disease, into a testimony that will affect not only your own life but the lives of thousands of others. That is precisely what He did for Dodie Osteen, the wife of John Osteen, pastor of Lakewood Church in Houston, Texas.

In the natural, this lady should have died years ago of cancer. Medical science had given up on her. The doctors said that she was a dead woman. But she wouldn't accept that verdict. She took the Word of God and fed on it day after day, night after night. She ingrained it deeply into her heart, just as I am urging you to do with these Scriptures I am giving you in this section. She spoke that Word out of her mouth. She held on to it. Come what may, she wouldn't let go of it for one minute. No matter how she felt or how things looked in the natural, she kept believing God and acting on His word of promise.

As a result, God completely healed her, so that she has been given a clean bill of health by the same medical experts who once were convinced that she was destined to die. Not only has that experience affected her own life, obviously, but it has affected the lives of thousands of other people around the world through her testimony. That's why I say that God can turn what seems to be a crisis in your life into a platform for a greater victory than you have ever experienced or could even imagine.

Notice in Deuteronomy 23:5 that God has the ability to turn a curse into a blessing. If that revelation ever gets into the spirit of the people of God, the devil hasn't got a chance. How can he? What kind of weapon does he have that can stand against such awesome power? How can he win if every time he tries to place a curse on any one of God's children, the Lord turns that curse into a blessing?

That's what Isaiah was referring to when he said: **No weapon that is formed against thee shall prosper; and every tongue that shall rise against thee in judgment thou shalt condemn.** *This is the heritage of the servants of the Lord,* **and their righteousness is of me, saith the Lord** (Is. 54:17).

All of my life I have heard people say, "It was a blessing in disguise." I used to wonder what they meant, but now I understand that expression perfectly. What they mean is what Joseph meant when he said to his jealous brothers who had betrayed him and sold him into slavery in Egypt: **But as for you, ye thought evil against me; but God meant it unto good, to bring to pass, as it is this day, to save much people alive** (Gen. 50:20). The *New International Version* translates this verse: **"You intended to harm me, but God intended it for good to accomplish what is now being done, the saving of many lives."**

No wonder the Apostle Paul kept on celebrating even in chains. No wonder he wrote to the believers in Corinth, **...Most gladly therefore will I rather glory in my infirmities, that the power of Christ may rest upon me** (2 Cor. 12:9). Paul could rejoice, give thanks, celebrate, and glory in the very midst of his worse trials and tribulations because he was aware of a truth that, sadly, most believers have not yet learned. He knew that every time the devil placed a curse upon him, God would turn it into a blessing.

That is the knowledge that I am trying desperately to get you to grasp. If you can ever get that concept securely fastened in your mind and heart, then nothing the devil throws at you will ever be able to shake you again. Like Paul, you will rejoice always, in every situation of life, because you will know that whatever the enemy brings against you God will turn to your advantage.

Mourning Turned to Joy

Then shall the virgin rejoice in the dance, both young men and old together: for I will *turn* their mourning into joy, and will comfort them, and make them rejoice from their sorrow.

Jeremiah 31:13

God says that He can turn mourning into joy. The Lord can turn tears of sorrow into tears of joy. An individual may go to bed in the evening weeping, but God can awaken him in the morning with rejoicing. (Ps. 30:5.)

What kind of defense does Satan have against such a person? He sends a curse upon an individual who says, "Praise God, I'm not worried; God will turn it into a blessing." He tries to attack a person with grief and sorrow, and God turns that grief and sorrow into joy and dancing. How can the devil win against such power? He can't.

In Psalm 30:11 David wrote of the Lord: **Thou hast** *turned* **for me my mourning into dancing: thou hast put off my sackcloth, and girded me with gladness.** Again we see that God has the power to turn mourning into dancing, sorrow into rejoicing, grief into gladness.

Captivity Turned to Laughter

When the Lord *turned* again the captivity of Zion, we were like them that dream.

Then was our mouth filled with laughter, and our tongue with singing: then said they among the heathen, The Lord hath done great things for them.

The Lord hath done great things for us; whereof we are glad.

Turn again our captivity, O Lord, as the streams in the south.

They that sow in tears shall reap in joy.

He that goeth forth and weepeth, bearing precious seed, shall doubtless come again with rejoicing, bringing his sheaves with him.

Psalm 126:1-6

If the Lord has ever turned anything in your life, He can do it again.

Here in this psalm David recalls how overjoyed the people were when the Lord turned the captivity of Israel. Then he goes on to ask the Lord to do once more what He has done in the past. David knew what I am sharing with you: what God has turned once, He can turn again.

Notice that David did not say *if* the Lord turns the captivity of Israel, he said *when* the Lord turns the captivity of Israel. What does that mean? It means that it's just a matter of time until the Lord does what He has promised to do.

Some people say to me, "Brother Jerry, what if...?" I say, "I don't deal with 'what ifs,' I deal with 'whens.'"

With God, it is always *when*, not *if*.

When the Lord turned the captivity of Israel, the people were so overjoyed they felt as if they were dreaming. One moment they were under pressure, not knowing how or when God was going to set them free of their bondage. The next moment, they were completely liberated. The miracle had come. The manifestation had been brought forth. The change was so complete and so sudden, it all seemed unreal. No wonder David writes that their mouths were filled with laughter and their tongues with singing.

I know that feeling. That kind of complete reversal of a bad situation has happened to me, and it is just as David describes. One moment you're down, and the next moment you're up. One moment you're lacking, and the next moment your need is met and there is even enough left over to help someone else. It *is* like a dream.

I remember one time not so long ago that my wife Carolyn and I were suddenly and unexpectedly faced with a tremendous need that we had not counted on at all. We had just returned from vacation, from two weeks of relaxing and recovering from our previous year's work, and were getting geared up for the new year and its challenges. We had not been back in the house two hours when suddenly the phone rang and we were abruptly informed that the ministry had to come up with a hundred thousand dollars by the end of the week — or else.

We were under extreme pressure. We were trusting God to meet all our needs, as always, but this was quite a shock. We had no idea where the funds were coming from, and no clue as to how to raise that kind of money in such a short time. In the natural, there was no way.

We just looked at one another and said, "Well, I guess we can sell all of our property and pay the debt." Then the Lord said, "Yes, but what are you going to sell next month?"

Carolyn and I had just built our dream home. We looked at each other and said, "Well, we can sell our house, put the money in the ministry, and pay off the debt." But it was Wednesday, and the money was due by Friday. That would have required a major miracle itself, to close the sale of a home in two days. But we were willing to do it, if that was what it took. We have always been agreeable to make any sacrifice necessary for the sake of ministry. We knew that God would get us another house.

But that wasn't God's best for us in that situation.

I remember that I lay down on one sofa in our garden room, and Carolyn lay down on another. Neither of us said a word. We just lay there.

Suddenly I jumped up and screamed at the top of my voice, "I don't deserve this! I've worked too hard, I've traveled too many miles, I've preached too many sermons, I've prayed too many prayers, I've given too much of myself to deserve this!"

That emotional outburst may have made me feel better, but it didn't impress the Lord at all. Nor did it move Him to take pity on me and say, "You poor thing, of course you don't deserve this. I'll tell you what Daddy's going to do, bless your heart. I'm going to get that mean ole money for you before noon, don't you worry."

Instead, I had to go over to my office and ask my accountant, "How much money have we got to pay on this debt?"

"None to speak of," he said. "We've used up nearly all the funds in the general account. We've paid the payroll, so there are no funds available from that source. In fact, we have nearly depleted all the accounts. All we have left is about ten thousand dollars."

To some people, ten thousand dollars may sound like a great deal of money, but when you need ten times that much, it's no help at all. So I called my attorney and explained the situation to him.

"I want you to handle this matter," I said. "We are going to pray and believe God. I don't know how it is going to happen, but you've been with this ministry long enough to know that we believe in miracles. You should, you've seen enough of them. Please take care of this for me."

"How much money have you got?" he asked.

"About ten thousand dollars," I answered.

"Okay," he responded, "I'll handle it."

He called the people we owed the money to. His opening words to them were: "Do you believe in miracles?" And this was a secular organization.

"No," they answered. "We don't have many of those around here."

"Well, I represent Jerry Savelle," he told them, "and I've been working with his ministry for many years. We do believe in miracles, and we believe that God is going to give us one. My client is a man of integrity. If he owes this money, then he will pay it. But it will take a miracle, you understand."

I like my attorney. He is a Word man.

"We have ten thousand dollars," he said. "We are going to send that much to you today. But we may need some time to come up with the rest of the amount. We believe in miracles, and when God provides, we will send the rest of your money to you."

"You have thirty days," they replied.

We got the money by Friday.

I called my attorney, waking him in the middle of the night.

"Hallelujah!" I said. "I've got the money!"

"You do?"

The next morning he got on the phone and called the lenders.

"Does anybody over there believe in miracles?" he asked.

"No," they answered. "We told you before that we don't see many of those around this place."

"Well, you've seen one now," he declared. "You gave us thirty days to pay our debt although it was due on Friday. We will be in today to pay it in full because we do believe in miracles."

As David said, it was like a dream. One moment we were in financial bondage, the next moment our financial captivity was turned. Then were our mouths filled with laughter, and our tongues were filled with singing. And the "heathen" (the staff of the secular company) was saying of us, "The Lord has done great things for them!"

What am I saying in all this? I am telling you that whatever the situation you may find yourself in at this moment, God can turn it around.

Do you feel like you are living under a curse? No problem. God can turn it into a blessing. Are you in captivity today? No problem. God can turn that captivity into freedom. Have you suffered a setback recently? No problem. God can turn that setback into a triumph.

Have you stumbled, have you fallen? No problem. Psalm 37:24 says of the righteous person: **Though he fall, he shall not be utterly cast down: for the Lord upholdeth him with his hand.** God will pick you up, dust you off, set you back on your feet, and give you a fresh start. He will fill your mouth with laughter and your tongue with singing. He will turn your situation so completely and so suddenly that the heathen will be amazed and will exclaim, "The Lord has done great things for them!"

Are you in any kind of captivity today? Then say out loud right now: "The Lord will turn again my captivity. He will fill my mouth with laughter and my tongue with singing. He will do great things for me, whereof I will be glad. Praise the Lord!"

5

Eye of Faith — Heart of Discipline

The Lord has shared with me on several occasions just how magnificent He is and how unlimited is His ability to turn things around for those who look to Him with expectant hearts. Over the years He has brought these points home to me in several dramatic ways.

For example, I remember some time ago I was flying to Tulsa, Oklahoma, from my home in Fort Worth, Texas, to speak at a ministerial conference. As I settled back into my airline seat for what is normally a fifty-to-fifty-five-minute flight, I began to meditate on what I was going to say in that meeting. As I did so I was suddenly reminded of a particular need my ministry was facing overseas.

A few days earlier, my international director who lives in Africa had called me and informed me that we needed twenty-five thousand dollars for a project in which we were involved. In the natural we did not have that amount of money because we had used up all our funds designated for African missions. The need was urgent, but we were in financial straits ourselves in our U.S. office.

So it was this pressing situation I was thinking about as I took my seat on the plane headed for Tulsa. Since my mind was on the subject, I mentioned it to the Lord in prayer. I just said, "Father, I need an extra twenty-five thousand dollars for our project in Kenya."

Instantly the Spirit of the Lord spoke to me and said, "When you get to Tulsa, a man and his wife will be coming to the meeting in which you are scheduled to minister. You don't know them; you've never even met them. They are involved in a ministry of distributing food to the poor. They need a large van to transport this food. At the meeting, when you stand up to speak, call these people forward and give them your van."

"But, Lord," I protested, "I didn't say anything about my van."

I had a van, a new one, but I had not brought up that subject. I wasn't even thinking about it. I was talking to God about *my* needs, not about the needs of some people I didn't even know.

So I got real quiet for a moment, and then I again brought up my need to the Lord.

"Father," I began, "let me talk to You about this need I have in Africa, this need for twenty-five thousand dollars."

But the Lord went right on talking. "When you get to Tulsa, there will be five preachers at the conference who are so discouraged, they are about to quit. They are coming to the meeting for a word from Me about what to do. If they don't get that word, they will leave the ministry, which is not My will. When you are at the pulpit, I want you to call these men forward and give each of them a suit of your clothes."

"But, Lord," I protested again, "I didn't say anything to You about my wardrobe. I'm talking about my need for twenty-five thousand dollars."

Again, He went on just as if He hadn't heard a word I said.

"There will be another minister there who is in dire financial need. I'm not asking you to meet his entire need, but I am asking you to plant a seed. Give him five hundred dollars."

"Lord, I don't want to talk to You any more," I answered. "Forget I ever brought up the subject of my need."

The reason I said that is because I know God. I knew what He was doing. He was opening the door for the miraculous. He does that to me quite often. In fact, it happens so often that it has become a lifestyle with my wife and me, as it should be for every believer.

How does this lifestyle work? Very simply. We talk to God about needs; He talks to us about seeds. We tell Him what we need, and He provides the answers to those needs by telling us where to plant seeds that will grow and produce fruit to supply the needs of others.

The Needs/Seeds Principle in Action

When I got to Tulsa, I went to the meeting, was introduced as the speaker, and began preaching. Suddenly about ten or fifteen minutes into my message, the Lord interrupted me and said, "Do it now."

So I stopped and declared, "There is a couple who has come here today. I don't know where you are from. I have never met you, but I know that you have a ministry distributing food to the poor. Would you please stand up?"

An older couple rose to their feet. I asked them to please come forward, which they did. I did not recognize them as anyone I had ever seen before. I asked them where they were from, and they said they were from Idaho.

"Well, while I was flying here today from Texas the Lord spoke to me and told me that you were in need of a large vehicle to transport the food you distribute. He said that you have been praying about this need for some time now. I just want you to know that I am the man who has your vehicle."

At that, they broke down and starting crying. Tears were just rolling down their faces.

"Are you going straight back to Idaho after this conference?" I asked them.

"No," they replied.

"Well, if you will go to Fort Worth with me, we will present that vehicle to you, and you can drive it back home with you."

They agreed enthusiastically and began to rejoice and praise the Lord.

Then, turning to the audience, I announced, "There are five preachers here who are about to leave the ministry. You have come here looking for a word of encouragement from the Lord. If you don't receive it, you are going to give up and quit. I would like for you to come forward at this time, please."

Immediately, five men got to their feet and moved to the front of the auditorium. What is amazing is that all five of them were just my size. So I told them what the Lord had said to me about them. I got their names and addresses, laid my hands on them, and prayed for them. Later, as soon as I got back home, I sent each of them one of my complete outfits: suit, shirt, tie, the works.

Finally, I ministered to the other person God had spoken to me about by planting five hundred dollars in his ministry.

Now that I had done my part, I got back on the airplane and flew back home.

Three days later I received a call in my office from a minister friend of mine.

"I've been praying, and God has been talking to me about your ministry," he said. "I believe I am supposed to plant twenty-five thousand dollars in your work in Africa."

The amazing thing is that I had never mentioned this need in that public meeting in Tulsa, nor had I revealed it to this man in private. When he told me that he felt that God had revealed to him that he was supposed to plant that money in my African ministry, I answered, "I don't doubt it a bit, brother. Send it on, praise the Lord!"

You see, I had talked to God about need, and He had talked to me about seed. Because I was faithful and obedient to plant that seed into the lives of others as a ministry to them, the Lord was faithful and obedient to His Word of promise to meet all my need in accordance to His riches in glory through Christ Jesus. Not only was my own need met, but the needs of others were also met in the process.

After that incident, I began to meditate on it. I thought about the infinite wisdom of God, how He has this unique ability to meet our needs, behind the scenes, in ways we know nothing about.

Here was a couple from Idaho who decided to come to Tulsa, Oklahoma, to attend a conference. Little did they know what was about to transpire there. In fact, they later revealed to me that they had misgivings about coming. It was very hard for them to do so because they thought they shouldn't be spending money going to a ministerial meeting. Instead, they figured that every dime should have been saved to go toward the purchase price of the vehicle they needed so desperately.

"Yet," they admitted, "the Lord kept impressing on us to go to Tulsa. If we had not been obedient to God, we would have missed our miracle."

What was so beautiful to me about this incident, is that God was in control of the entire operation from beginning to end. From His unique position, He could see Idaho and Texas at the same time. That couple up in Idaho had no way of knowing that at the moment of their greatest need, the

Lord was speaking to a man down in Texas, who was on an airplane between Fort Worth and Tulsa, instructing him to meet their need.

That's why I say that you and I should never give up. We never know what God has worked out for our need to be met. Just as He could speak to a couple in Idaho and a man in Texas and have them meet in Oklahoma so their needs would be met, He can work in any set of circumstances to bring answers and solutions to all kinds of seemingly hopeless situations — behind the scenes.

The Third Eye

Are they [angels] not all ministering spirits, sent forth to minister for them who shall be heirs of salvation?

Hebrews 1:14

The reason I say that God can work "behind the scenes," is because there is another realm of existence besides the natural realm in which the world operates on a daily basis. In that other realm there are angels — ministering spirits — who are sent by God to work on our behalf.

If the Lord were to open our eyes so that we could truly see what is going on in this invisible spiritual realm, we would see the multitudes of angelic beings who have been assigned to us by the Lord. They are there for the specific purpose of ministering to us in our day-to-day lives.

In many ways and forms, God is at work right now changing things, realigning events, adjusting circumstances, influencing people in order to meet our needs. That's the reason that the Apostle Paul could say with such absolute finality, "I *know* that this situation will turn to my salvation." He was saying, "I know that there is a higher realm than what meets the eye. There is something going on in the unseen world that will work to my deliverance."

As believers, you and I have been blessed with the same privilege that the Apostle Paul enjoyed. Like Paul, we are not limited to what we can see with our natural eyes. As new spiritual creatures, we can also see with spiritual eyes. That is, we can see into the unseen realm.

This ability to see the solution to a situation which is beyond the natural ability to perceive is what I call "the third eye."

Thank God that we have this "third eye," the eye of faith, that can see what others cannot see, that can look into a realm that others cannot perceive. If the world tells them that it is all over, they accept what they are told because that's all they know. But when the world tells us that it is all over, we can laugh and reply, "You say that because you don't see what I see; you don't know what I know."

That's why we should never give up, regardless of our outward circumstances. Even when we are under pressure, we should refuse to surrender.

I learned a long time ago that when I am under the greatest pressure to quit, that is always an indication that Satan has just fired his best shot. If he didn't get me with that one, then he is finished.

So if you are under great pressure today, it is time to rejoice. If you think you can't possibly hold on any longer, if you are left wobbling on one leg, then take joy; the devil has just launched his fiercest attack, and you are still standing.

Notice that Paul didn't say that he thought he would be delivered, or that he hoped he would be delivered, or that he prayed he would be delivered; instead, he said that he *knew* he would be delivered. You can know that too. When you get out of the realm of wondering and into the realm of knowing, you will discover the greatest joy you will ever experience in your life.

Like the Apostle Paul, like David of old, I *know* that I will be delivered from all my afflictions.

"How do you know?"

Because the Bible tells me so.

"But I need something deeper, something more solid, something more concrete, than that."

There is nothing deeper or more solid or more concrete than the Word of God.

In speaking of his life-or-death situation, Paul could say, "I *know* that this will turn."

That is what you should be saying in your situation, whatever it may be: "I know that this will turn." Say it as though you mean it: "I *know* that this will turn." Now say it so that the devil will know you mean it: "I *know* that this *will* turn!"

If you will make that profession of faith a practice until it becomes your habitual response to whatever situation you find yourself facing, you will not go on oppressed, depressed, or dejected. You will go on with a smile on your face and a joy in your heart that others cannot understand. You will go through life talking faith, because you will be able to see with the eye of faith — the "third eye" that looks not at the seen but at the unseen, not at the temporal but at the eternal. (2 Cor. 4:18.)

The Choice Is Yours

And be not conformed to this world, but be ye transformed by the renewing of your mind....
Romans 12:2

We have seen that because the Apostle Paul knew the power of prayer and of earnest expectation and hope, he knew how to tap into the supernatural ability of the Holy Ghost. Paul understood the vital role that attitude plays in success. That is why he was always so positive in his words and actions.

The same must be true of us. We shouldn't expect to fail, we should expect to succeed. We shouldn't expect to be laid off from work, we should expect to be promoted and given a raise. We shouldn't expect to stay sick, we should expect to get well. If everyone on our street comes down with the flu, we shouldn't expect to be next. Instead, we should expect to be the only one on the block who doesn't get the flu.

It is just as easy to be positive as it is to be negative. It is just as easy to go forward as it is to go backward.

Did you ever notice that your automobile has a forward gear and a reverse gear — and between them a neutral gear? Do you know why neutral is there? To give you an opportunity to make a decision as to which direction you would like to go. It takes no more energy to go forward than it does to go backward. The procedure for going forward is exactly the same as for going in reverse. The vital difference is in the decision process.

The authority to make decisions has been given to us by the Lord. We determine which direction our life will ultimately take. The choice is ours. We decide, by an act of our will. No one, not even Satan, has the right to usurp authority over our will. No one, including the devil, can force us to go backward if we have decided to go forward.

You and I can choose to be positive just as we can choose to be negative, just as we can choose to go forward or backward. The sad thing is that most Christians spend their life going backward instead of forward. Many never even get out of neutral. The reason they do that is because they have been taught to be indecisive, to be negative. That's why Paul tells us that we must be transformed by the renewing of our minds.

Someone will say, "Yes, but what if being positive doesn't work?"

My answer to that question is, "Yes, but what if it does work?"

You see, I can be just as positive as others are negative.

Others may choose to go through life in reverse gear, but I choose to go forward. So should you. After reading these pages, you should be filled with great hope and expectation. From this moment on you should expect God to do the impossible in your situation — whatever that situation may be. You should expect God to exalt you and promote you even though everyone else is being demoted or laid off. You should expect God to keep you well even though everyone else is getting sick. You should expect God to prosper you even though everyone else is going bankrupt. You should expect God to bless your marriage even though everyone else is getting a divorce. You should expect God to deliver your children even though everyone else's kids seem to be sinking deeper into sin and rebellion.

"But, brother, aren't you just building up people's hopes?"

That's my job. Someone has to do it. There are enough negative influences in this world today. We need someone to put in a good word. There are enough hopeless people in our society. We need someone who is filled with hope and positive expectation. That is what I have been called to do and to be for this generation. And so have you. You can be positive or you can be negative.

The choice is yours.

The Lifestyle of Discipline

Is any sick among you? let him call for the elders of the church; and let them pray over him, anointing him with oil in the name of the Lord:

> And the prayer of faith shall save the sick, and the Lord shall raise him up; and if he have committed sins, they shall be forgiven him.
>
> **James 5:14,15**
>
> ...they shall lay hands on the sick, and they shall recover.
>
> **Mark 16:18**

Paul made his choice. Instead of becoming negative, he chose to be positive. Instead of becoming hopeless, he gave thanks to God Who always caused him to triumph.

If you and I are not triumphing, it is not God's fault. Just as He caused Paul always to triumph, so He will cause us always to triumph — if we will display the same attitude in our situation that Paul displayed in his. It may not happen overnight, but it will happen — if we persevere.

The problem with most Charismatic Christians is that they are not disciplined. Many came into the Charismatic Movement because it looked to be a place where anything goes. They seem to have the mistaken idea that commitment is bondage. Commitment and dedication and discipline are not bondage, they are a vital part of the Christian life.

We Charismatics love to boast of our "freedom." Often what that means is that we love having no demands placed upon us. We love to hear sermons on how to prosper and be successful. What we don't like to hear is that prosperity and success depend on discipline. We like our Christianity to be comfortable. We don't want to face the fact that anything worthwhile requires patience and perseverance.

If we pray for healing and then stand in faith for three days without seeing any results, we are ready to give up and decide that "this faith thing doesn't work." Yet, we will follow our doctor's prescriptions for days or even weeks on end without seeing any change in our condition.

If our personal physician orders us to take some pills twice a day for the next seven days, assuring us that at the end of that time we will be well, we will do exactly as he says, fully expecting the healing process to take a whole week. We would never think of not taking our medicine the full time period. We would never take it for a couple of days and then throw it away, claiming, "This stuff doesn't work!"

Yet when someone lays hands on us and prays for our healing in accordance with the Word of God, if we don't see instant results, we conclude that prayer and faith don't work.

The Word of God says that if anyone is sick, he should call for the elders of the church to pray for him, and the prayer of faith *shall* save him. Jesus said that those who believe in Him shall lay hands on the sick, and they *shall* recover. We are told that they shall recover, but we are not told *when* they shall recover. Some recover instantly. Some recover in a week. Some recover in a month. Some recover in a year.

The healing process by prayer and faith may take just as long as the healing process by medicine and therapy. In both cases, the patient (one who exercises *patience*) must be disciplined if he is to recover.

In Proverbs 4:20-22 the Lord tells us what we must do while we are waiting for our recovery by prayer and faith:

> **My son, attend to my words; incline thine ear unto my sayings.**
>
> **Let them not depart from thine eyes; keep them in the midst of thine heart.**
>
> **For they are life unto those that find them, and health to all their flesh.**

God's Word is our medicine. If we will take a healthy dose of it every day, we will recover. But because we are so undisciplined, we want this recovery to be manifested instantaneously, and without any demands on us. If it doesn't happen that way, then we don't have any faith or confidence in the spiritual healing process.

I wish someone would discover a way to stay physically trim and fit without dieting and exercise. But that plan does not exist.

I know how hard it is to follow a healthy regime of proper nutrition and regular exercise, especially since I am on the road traveling so much. When I get back to my hotel room in some strange city after a long day of travel and ministry, the last thing I want to do is work out. And the last thing I want to eat is a rice cake and a plate of broccoli, especially when the neon signs up and down the street are all beckoning me to pizza parlors and fast food joints.

I have a friend named Dennis Tinerino, a former Mr. Universe. He is immaculate in appearance. He looks as if he was chiseled out of stone. Since I have put on a few pounds here and there over the years, Dennis decided to come visit me for a few days in order to put me on a program of proper diet and exercise, including weight lifting and early morning workouts.

The first day when the alarm went off at 5:30 A.M., I jumped out of bed. The second day I was so sore I could hardly move. Needless to say, when I finished each day's workout, I really wasn't interested in health foods. But Dennis had denied me what I really wanted: Mexican food, junk food, and lots of it. Day after day he kept me honest, insisting that I follow the program to the letter, promising me that in thirty days' time I wouldn't recognize myself when I looked in the mirror.

Finally, the period of his instructional visit came to an end, and I took Dennis to the airport to catch a plane back home. As soon as that aircraft left the ground, I got in my car and began driving home. Now in Texas we have some of the best Mexican restaurants in the world, and I am especially partial to that kind of food. Between the

Dallas/Fort Worth airport and my house I must have passed no less than fifty great restaurants. I felt as if I hadn't had anything to eat for days. My intentions were good. I was going to pass right by all these places and pay them no attention whatsoever. I kept looking straight ahead. But then out of the corner of my eye I saw a sign for one of my favorite Mexican restaurants. I could see it, I could smell it, and I could even hear it — melodious South-of-the-Border voices coming from that delicious-smelling building crying out to me, "Hey, señor, we've got some enchiladas for you. Come on in and enjoy yourself."

Despite my best intentions, I suddenly wheeled into that restaurant, sat down at a table, and ordered everything on the first page — for starters. Later when I got back home I looked at myself in the mirror and said, "You don't look so bad, boy. Forget those rice cakes. Get rid of those jogging suits. Sell all that exercise equipment in the garage."

What happened? I had good intentions, but no discipline. That reveals a weakness in my character.

What did I do? I compromised. I bought bigger suits. I tried to hide my fat behind layers of cloth. But then there finally came a time when I said, "No, I'm not wearing those 'fat suits' any longer! I am not going to allow my physical appetite to control my life."

Now I still have to work at my weight continuously, something I never had to do when I was younger. When I first went to work for Brother Kenneth Copeland over twenty years ago, I weighed 120 pounds. I was so skinny that you could count my ribs — through my T-shirt! I was so thin that if I stood sideways I didn't even cast a shadow. Never in my wildest dreams did I ever foresee myself having an ounce of fat on my emaciated Barney Fife body. I thought I would never have to deal with diets and exercise machines.

Then one day when I got be about thirty-five years old, all of a sudden everything changed. It seemed that everything I ate turned into instant fat. I realized that if I didn't do something quick I would soon get to the place that I couldn't squeeze through the door. I had to take a stand, to take control of my physical body and its appetites. And I realized that no one else could do it for me.

The same is true spiritually. Just as we must be disciplined in our natural walk, so we must be disciplined in the walk of faith. It is fine to go to church, get "hyped up," and make wonderful resolutions. But unless we are willing to follow through on those resolutions, it is all for nothing. It is after the meeting is over, in the normal day-by-day grind of everyday living, that we discover whether what we have experienced is true spiritual inspiration or just good intentions.

Faith cannot be a feeling. It cannot be an experience. It cannot be a movement. It has got to be a lifestyle. Obviously, to follow this lifestyle on a regular daily basis requires a great deal of self-motivation and self-discipline. We cannot look to others to provide either of these things for us.

It is so easy to be moved by what we see or hear, to be influenced by the masses who do not live by the Word and will of God. That's the reason it takes strong discipline to follow this lifestyle. But in the end, it is well worth it when we see God honor our faithfulness by turning our dismal captivity into glorious freedom.

6
The Fourth Man

God is not looking for people who have it all together so He can make disciples of them. Study God's track record. Usually He picks those who are least likely, those who have nothing going for them in the natural.

If I had been Jesus, I would never have picked Simon the fisherman as my disciple. The man was a hothead and a boaster who went around shooting off his mouth without the ability to back up what he said by action.

But obviously Jesus is not like you and me. What did He do? He chose a bigmouth braggart who was destined to deny Him three times in public, and transformed him into a tower of strength who preached powerful sermons and worked mighty miracles. He took a compromiser and transformed him into a crusader. He took Simon (whose name meant "reed") and transformed him into Peter (whose name meant "rock").

If God can take a reed and turn it into a rock, then there is hope for you and me.

Captivity Turned, Life Restored

...the Lord thy God will *turn thy captivity*, and have compassion upon thee, and will return and gather thee from all the nations....

If any of thine be driven out unto the outmost parts of heaven, from thence will the Lord thy God gather thee, and from thence will he fetch thee:

83

And the Lord thy God will bring thee into the land which thy fathers possessed, and thou shalt possess it; and he will do thee good, and multiply thee above thy fathers.

And the Lord thy God will circumcise thine heart, and the heart of thy seed, to love the Lord thy God with all thine heart, and with all thy soul, that thou mayest live.

Deuteronomy 30:3-6

As we have seen, God is a master at turning failures into champions, curses into blessings, mourning into joy, weeping into dancing, sackcloth into garments of gladness, slavery into freedom.

God's ability never ceases to amaze me. He has the marvelous capacity to take people who are being held in bondage and turn their captivity. He can turn their exile and bring them into the land that their fathers possessed, there to do them good and to multiply them all the days of their lives. He can take the people who in the natural are the least likely to succeed, and cause them to flourish and prosper.

If He can do all that, God can turn your captivity into freedom. He can elevate you to a level of position you have never known before. I know this is true from personal experience.

Do you realize that in 1969 I was a body man. I repaired wrecked automobiles. That was my profession. I owned my own auto body repair shop. That's what my father had done before me, and that was what I had always envisioned myself doing. It was the height of my ambition in life. And I loved it.

But in that year I answered the call of God that I first heard at the age of twelve. Even then Carolyn and I had no idea what that surrender would mean in our lives. You must realize that my wife and I were just simple, middle-class country people. We didn't come from wealthy families, although they were good, honest, God-fearing people. We never dreamed that we would ever travel around the world. We assumed that we would spend the rest of our days in rural Louisiana where we had grown up. Every once in a while we might go to Texas, to Mississippi, Oklahoma, or Arkansas. But that was about the extent of our travels — a five-state area. Never did we dream that we would see California, New York, or Montana. I read about such places and thought how wonderful they must be, but never in my wildest imagination did I think I would ever see them myself.

England, Europe, Africa, Asia, Australia? Just faraway places with strange-sounding names.

But I answered the call of the Lord on my life, willing to follow wherever He might lead. If that meant staying in Louisiana for the rest of my life, so be it.

One night in church at the end of the service, the guest speaker asked all the men in attendance to come forward and allow him and the pastor to minister to them. I got in line with the other men of the church and eventually made my way to the front where the two ministers were laying hands on each man and speaking a word of prophecy over him. When I knelt in front of them, one of them began saying, "Airplanes, airplanes, airplanes; fly, fly, fly; airplanes, airplanes, airplanes. Oh, Jerry, you are going to be flying all the time."

That was news to me. But since I was so young in the Lord I just took it in stride and went on my way, thinking little of it.

Today, over two decades later, I fly constantly. I have been all over the world. I have never visited a nation on the face of the earth as a stranger. By the time I arrive, my tapes and books have preceded me by years. People begin coming to me at the airport, calling my name and quoting the titles of my books and sermons and tapes.

I have been in a mud hut in the middle of the African bush with no electricity or running water and have looked down and seen one of my books lying there. In that kind of situation, I always wonder, "How did that get here? For that matter, how did I get here?" Then I remember. I got there by surrendering my life to the will of God.

What am I saying by all this? I am saying that God's hand is on you just as much as it is on me. You may not be called to one of the offices of ministry in which I function, but you are loved and called by God just as much as I am. God has a plan for your life, and you would be a fool to limit Him.

Whatever your situation, no matter how hopeless it may appear, you are not out of God's reach. He can turn your captivity and elevate you to heights you could never even imagine — just as He has done for me and so many others like me. Why? Because God is a master at making champions out of failures.

They Serve Not Thy Gods

Wherefore at that time certain Chaldeans came near, and accused the Jews.

They spake and said to the king Nebuchadnezzar, O king, live for ever.

Thou, O king, has made a decree, that every man that shall hear the sound of the cornet, flute, harp, sackbut, psaltery, and dulcimer, and all kinds of musick, shall fall down and worship the golden image:

And whoso falleth not down and worshippeth, that he should be cast into the midst of a burning fiery furnace.

There are certain Jews whom thou hast set over the affairs of the province of Babylon, Shadrach, Meshach,

and Abednego; these men, O king, have not regarded
thee: they serve not thy gods, nor worship the golden
image which thou hast set up.

Daniel 3:8-12

I am sure you recognize this passage. It is one of my all-
time favorite stories in the Bible because it illustrates so
well God's mighty power to turn a crisis situation into a
glorious triumph.

As our story begins, we see that "certain Chaldeans,"
jealous of the royal favor showered on Shadrach, Meshach,
and Abednego, have informed King Nebuchadnezzar that
these three, his most trusted Jewish officials, have failed to
comply with the law of the land which requires worship of
the golden image set up by him. Obviously, as we see, this
is a serious offense, one punishable by death.

Our God Is Able, and
He Will Deliver Us

Then Nebuchadnezzar in his rage and fury
commanded to bring Shadrach, Meshach, and
Abednego. They then brought these men before the
king.

Nebuchadnezzar spake and said unto them, Is it
true, O Shadrach, Meshach, and Abednego, do not ye
serve my gods, nor worship the golden image which I
have set up?

Now if ye be ready that at what time ye hear the
sound of the cornet, flute, harp, sackbut, psaltery, and
dulcimer, and all kinds of musick, ye fall down and
worship the image which I have made; well: but if ye
worship not, ye shall be cast the same hour into the
midst of a burning fiery furnace; and who is that God
that shall deliver you out of my hands?

Shadrach, Meshach, and Abednego, answered and
said to the king, O Nebuchadnezzar, we are not careful
to answer thee in this matter.

87

> If it be so, our God whom we serve is able to deliver us from the burning fiery furnace, and he will deliver us out of thine hand, O king.
>
> But if not, be it known unto thee, O king, that we will not serve thy gods, nor worship the golden image which thou hast set up.
>
> Daniel 3:13-18

Notice the pride and arrogance of King Nebuchadnezzar. He is incensed that anyone, even his most trusted officials, would dare to defy his decree. He has them brought before him and demands to know what kind of God they think they serve Who can save them from his royal hands.

You may be facing the same type of situation as these faithful servants of the Lord. Perhaps the prince of this world is angry at you and screaming in your head right now, "Where is your God? What makes you think that He can change what the government (or the bank or the mortgage company or the medical profession) has decreed?"

The devil loves to scream at people: "Where is your God? Where is the Lord you trust so much now that you need Him? Where is He when you are declared incurable by the doctors? Where is He when you are declared insolvent by the bank? Where is He when your children are declared guilty by the courts? Who is that God that will deliver you out of my hands?"

Shadrach, Meshach, and Abednego were not impressed or intimidated by the king's questions. They knew exactly where their God was and were convinced that He was just as aware of where they were and what they were facing. They had the greatest confidence that He would deliver them. That's why they could exercise such holy boldness in answering the king: "If it so be, our God whom we serve is able to deliver us from the burning fiery furnace, and He will deliver us."

88

Anyone can say, "Our God is able." But when he has the audacity to say, "And He *will* deliver me," then he has stepped out where few people dare to tread.

Then Shadrach, Meshach, and Abednego went on to tell the king, "But even if our God doesn't deliver us, we still refuse to bow down to your golden image or to worship your heathen gods."

When the Hebrew children told the king all these things, it made him furious, just as it makes our enemy furious when we stand up to his accusations.

There Is Always a Way!

Then was Nebuchadnezzar full of fury, and the form of his visage was changed against Shadrach, Meshach, and Abednego: therefore he spake, and commanded that they should heat the furnace one seven times more than it was wont to be heated.

And he commanded the most mighty men that were in his army to bind Shadrach, Meshach, and Abednego, and to cast them into the burning fiery furnace.

Then these men were bound in their coats, their hosen, and their hats, and their other garments, and were cast into the midst of the burning fiery furnace.

Therefore because the king's commandment was urgent, and the furnace exceeding hot, the flame of the fire slew those men that took up Shadrach, Meshach, and Abednego.

And these three men, Shadrach, Meshach, and Abednego, fell down bound into the midst of the burning fiery furnace.

Daniel 3:19-23

When these three young men were thrown into the fiery furnace, they were totally helpless. In the natural, there was no hope for them. I think this is a beautiful picture of reliance upon the supernatural power of God.

When man has absolutely no way in the natural to free himself from the fiery furnace into which he has been cast by the enemy, God can still turn that situation around. If these men had not been bound hand and foot, they might have been able to run out of the flames. But there was not even that slight chance of escape. There was no human source on which to lean. They could not rely on the arm of flesh because there was none to rely on. They were totally and completely helpless.

That may be the way you feel today. That may be what the medical profession has told you; that you are bound and helpless, with no way out of your dilemma. That may be what you have been told by the financial institution or the Internal Revenue Service or the judicial system; that there is no way out for you.

Let me tell you something: as long as Jesus is Lord, as long as He is still seated on His throne in heaven, there *is* a way, there is *always* a way!

For the Hebrew children that way was not *out of* the burning fiery furnace, but *through* it. But even then God saw to it that they did not have to go through it alone.

The Fourth Man

Then Nebuchadnezzar the king was astonied, and rose up in haste, and spake, and said unto his counsellers, Did not we cast three men bound into the midst of the fire? They answered and said unto the king, True, O king.

He answered and said, Lo, I see four men loose, walking in the midst of the fire, and they have no hurt; and the form of the fourth is like the Son of God.

Daniel 3:24,25

Not only did the king see four men in the fiery furnace, but he saw that they were loose.

God was not responsible for having these men bound, but He was responsible for setting them free of their bonds.

God did not heat up the fire, but He did cause it to lose its power. God did not cast these men into the furnace, but He did protect them and give them freedom in the very midst of it.

Notice that these three men — now become four men — were loose and walking about, in no apparent hurry to get out of the furnace. Now this is the same furnace whose flames had been heated seven times hotter than usual. If these men could be totally confident that their God would deliver them, if they could walk about in a fire seven times hotter than any known before, then surely you and I can stand against the devil and declare as they did, "I will not bow, and I will not burn!"

These men were operating under the old covenant. The book of Hebrews tells us that we have a better covenant based on better promises. (Heb. 8:6.) If these men could "wax bold" and "do exploits" under the old covenant, then surely you and I can do the same under the new covenant.

But notice that there was a fourth man in that "burning fiery furnace." King Nebuchadnezzar was astonished that this fourth man was there in that situation. But if you will read your Bible, you will find this fourth man showing up every time there is a people who will not bow. He shows up in Daniel's lions' den. He shows up at Moses' Red Sea. He shows up at Elijah's River Jordan. He shows up in Stephen's stoning. He shows up on every page from Genesis to Revelation.

He is the alpha and the omega, the beginning and the end. He has always showed up throughout the history of mankind, and He is about to show up again, very soon. Not only will He show up in your fiery furnace and mine, but He is about to show up before the nations. He is about to split the clouds and shout, "Come up hither!" (Rev. 4:1.)

Who is this fourth man? Well, I know of no one who describes Him better than Oral Roberts. Brother Roberts says: In Genesis He is the seed of woman. In Exodus He is the passover lamb. In Leviticus He is the high priest. In Numbers He is the pillar of cloud by day and the pillar of fire by night. In Deuteronomy He is the prophet likened to Moses. In Joshua He is the captain of our salvation.

In Judges He is the judge and lawgiver. In Ruth He is our kinsman-redeemer. In First and Second Samuel He is the trusted prophet. In First and Second Kings and Chronicles He is the reigning king.

In Ezra He is the faithful scribe. In Nehemiah He is the rebuilder of the broken-down walls of human life. In Esther He is our Mordecai. In Job He is the everliving redeemer.

Who is this fourth man? In Psalms He is our shepherd. In Proverbs and Ecclesiastes He is our wisdom. In the Song of Solomon He is our lover and our bridegroom.

In Isaiah He is the prince of peace. In Jeremiah He is the righteous branch. In Lamentations He is the weeping prophet. In Ezekiel He is the wonderful four-faced man. And in Daniel He is the fourth man in life's fiery furnace.

Who is this fourth man? In Hosea He is the faithful husband. In Joel He is the baptizer in the Holy Ghost and fire. In Amos He is the burden-bearer. In Obadiah He is mighty to save. In Jonah He is our great foreign missionary. In Micah He is the messenger with beautiful feet.

In Nahum He is the avenger of God's elect. In Habakkuk He is God's evangelist. In Zephaniah He is our savior. In Haggai He is the restorer of God's lost heritage. In Zechariah He is the fountain in the house of David for sin and uncleanness. In Malachi He is the sun of righteousness rising with healing in His wings.

Who is this fourth man? In Matthew He is the Messiah. In Mark He is the wonder-worker. In Luke He is the Son of Man. In John He is the Son of God.

In Acts He is the Holy Ghost. In Romans He is our justifier. In First and Second Corinthians He is our sanctifier. In Galatians He is the redeemer from the curse of the law. In Ephesians He is the Christ of unsearchable riches. In Philippians He is the God Who supplies all of our need. In Colossians He is the fullness of the Godhead bodily.

Who is this fourth man? In First and Second Thessalonians He is our soon-coming king. In First and Second Timothy He is the mediator between God and man. In Titus He is the faithful pastor. In Philemon He is the beloved brother.

Who is this fourth man? In Hebrews He is the blood of the everlasting covenant. In James He is the great physician. In First and Second Peter He is the chief shepherd. In First, Second, and Third John He is love. In Jude He is the Lord Jesus coming with ten thousand of His saints.

Who is this fourth man? In Revelation He is the King of kings and the Lord of lords. Hallelujah!

Who is this fourth man? He is Abel's sacrifice, Noah's rainbow, Abraham's ram, Isaac's wells, Jacob's scepter, Moses' rod, Joshua's sun and moon that stood still, Elijah's mantle, Elisha's staff, Gideon's fleece, Samuel's horn of oil, David's slingshot, Hezekiah's sun dial, Daniel's vision, Amos' burden, and Malachi's sun of righteousness.

He is Peter's shadow, Stephen's signs and wonders, Paul's handkerchief and aprons, John's pearly white city.

He is father to the orphan, husband to the widow. To the traveler in the night He is the bright and morning star. To those who walk through the lonesome valley, He is the lily of the valley, the rose of Sharon, and the honey in the rock.

Who is this fourth man? He is the brightness of God's glory. He is the express image of the person of God. He is the pearl of great price. He is the rock in a weary land, the cup that runneth over, the rod and staff that comfort.

Who is this fourth man? He is Jesus of Nazareth, the Son of the Living God, hallelujah![1]

And He is the One Who can turn things around — for you!

[1]Oral Roberts, *Best-Loved Tent Sermons* (Tulsa: Oral Roberts, 1983), pp. 16-18 lightly paraphrased. Used by permission.

7
Spiritual Laws of Prosperity

And this is the confidence that we have in him [God], that, if we ask any thing according to his will, he heareth us:

And if we know that he hear us, whatsoever we ask, we know that we have the petitions that we desired of him.

1 John 5:14,15

Years ago Oral Roberts used to say at the close of each of his broadcasts, "Something good is going to happen to you!"

Some Christians became upset with him for making that statement.

"How does he know that something good is going to happen to me?" they asked. "He doesn't even know me."

Of course, the answer is that Oral Roberts wasn't talking to them. He was talking to those who prayed and believed, those who, like the Apostle Paul, fully expected God to answer their prayers, to intervene in their situation, and to do something about it.

But, as we have seen, the kind of solid hope and earnest expectation that marked the life of Paul is the result of a lifestyle of close communion and fellowship with God. Paul could display such confidence in spite of his current circumstances because he knew Whom he believed. (2 Tim. 1:12.) He knew that his God would hear and answer prayer on his behalf.

The basic message to be learned here is: *If you can pray, your situation can turn.*

There is power in prayer. There is also a great deal of wonderful teaching on this subject today, especially in the United States. Brother Kenneth Copeland has produced some excellent messages on how to build and develop an accurate prayer life. Brother Kenneth Hagin also offers an outstanding series on seven steps to prayer that brings results.

If you want something good to happen to you, if you want to follow a lifestyle of hope and earnest expectation, then learn to pray. Learn to have confidence that when you pray, God hears, heaven moves, and hell shutters. Learn to do as the Apostle Paul did: to pray and to tap into the awesome, limitless power of the Holy Ghost. Then also do as Paul did and give thanks to God Who always causes you to triumph.

Failure Is Not Fatal

...and, lo, I am with you alway, even unto the end of the world....
Matthew 28:20

In the mind of God, no situation in your life is ever over until you triumph over it. But remember, that triumph may not be manifest overnight. If you will do as the Hebrew children and refuse to bow, you will not burn. If you will stand your ground, and having done all to stand, then God will stand with you — even in the midst of the fiery furnace. The fourth man will go with you through any situation and over any obstacle until you are triumphant.

In His Word, God has promised never to leave us or forsake us. (Heb. 13:5.) God is willing to go to any length to see us through to victory. He won't give up, give out, or give in. He won't jump ship, even if the ship is sinking. If we will remain faithful and strong, if we will hold fast to our hope and our earnest expectation, then God will do His part and cause us to triumph in every situation of life.

God knows nothing of a win-a-few, lose-a-few philosophy. I don't follow that philosophy either. As a child of the Living God, I believe I have a right to triumph always.

"Do you mean to tell me that you never have any setbacks?"

I didn't say that.

"Do you mean that you have never failed?"

I didn't say that either. In fact, I have had and continue to have my share of what the world would call failures. But I don't call them failures. I call them temporary transitions.

Despite my setbacks and "temporary transitions," I am not a failure until I say I am a failure. The same is true of you. You are not a failure until you accept failure as the final word.

We all know the story of Thomas Edison who tried hundreds of filaments before finding one that would work in his new invention, the light bulb. Despite his many "failures," he didn't give up until he was successful. As a result, you and I live in the light of a new electronic era.

When Henry Ford made his first automobile, he forgot to put in it a reverse gear. But he didn't quit. He didn't give up just because he was less than totally successful the first time. Today, people drive effortlessly across whole continents because visionaries like Henry Ford refused to be daunted by the obstacles and rebuffs they encountered on the way to success.

The Wright brothers were told repeatedly that their flying machine would never get off the ground. But they wouldn't listen, and they wouldn't give up. Their experimental aircraft did get off the ground. Although the length of its maiden flight was less than the overall length of a modern-day super airliner, it was still a tremendous step forward. In fact, it made aviation history. Today hundreds of travelers at a time fly in pressurized comfort across wide oceans because two bicycle mechanics from Ohio would not give up on a dream.

That never-say-die spirit is exactly the kind of attitude that God is looking for in His people today. As His intrepid spiritual explorers and adventurers, we need to become success-minded, win-minded, triumph-minded. If we suffer a setback, that doesn't mean that our life is over. It just means that we must pick ourselves up, dust ourselves off, get back in the Word of God, and start anew.

With the help of God, any situation can be turned around. In the final pages of this book, I would like to deal with turning a financial crisis into a financial miracle. To do that, I will share with you several spiritual laws of divine prosperity. These laws begin with the tithe. ✓

The Rewards of the Tither

Bring ye all the tithes into the storehouse, that there may be meat in mine house, and prove me now herewith, saith the Lord of hosts, if I will not open you the windows of heaven, and pour you out a blessing, that there shall not be room enough to receive it.

And I will rebuke the devourer for your sakes, and he shall not destroy the fruits of your ground; neither shall your vine cast her fruit before the time in the field, saith the Lord of hosts.

And all nations shall call you blessed: for ye shall be a delightsome land, saith the Lord of hosts.

Malachi 3:10-12

In the *King James Version* where the Lord says, "I will open to you the windows of heaven and pour you out a blessing, that there shall not be room enough to receive it," another translation says, **I will open the windows of heaven for you and pour out blessings for you until you shall say, It is enough.**[1]

Have you been blessed yet by the Lord so much that you have had to shout to Him, "That's enough!"? Neither have I. But nevertheless, today I believe this word from the Lord. That was not always the case. I used to wonder about that passage in Malachi. I even spoke to some great preachers about it.

I remember one time when Oral Roberts came to speak at one of our mission conferences in Fort Worth, Texas. In that meeting he shared with us that every morning he had to get up and face the task of believing God for four hundred thousand dollars to come in before the sun went down. That was the daily amount it took to keep his ministry going in those days. I am sure it must be much more than that now.

Then Brother Roberts went on to say, "That is one thought away from insanity. If I start thinking the wrong way, I know I will have to be carried off to a padded room somewhere."

Can you imagine having to believe God for four hundred thousand dollars every day of your life? If Oral Roberts could do that for years on end, then surely you and I can believe God for what we need day by day.

When I first began to get involved in the Word of Faith, I thought that Christians had to talk God into meeting their needs financially. I thought that if a person got "good enough," then God might agree to meet his material needs. I had picked up that mistaken idea somewhere in my earlier years. Still I wasn't sure how to go about it.

---

[1]George M. Lamsa, *The Holy Bible: From Ancient Eastern Manuscripts* (Nashville: Holman Bible Publishers, 1933, 1939, 1940, 1957, 1961, 1967, 1968 by A. J. Holman Co.), p. 947.

I remember questioning Brother Kenneth Copeland about this matter the second time he came to my hometown. In those days I was struggling with my finances and with God's way of dealing with this issue. I had no problem believing God for healing. That was simple to me. I just accepted that divine health was part of God's provision for His children, believed for it, and walked in it.

But for some reason, getting my financial needs met was about to drive me up the wall. I was deep in debt before I finally discovered that God would supply all my need through His riches in Christ Jesus.

As it turned out, Brother Copeland had a slight accident in his car on that trip, and since I had been in the auto body repair business in the past, he asked me if I would repair his car while he was in town. So I agreed.

One day he came over to watch me work. As he did so, he began asking me questions about what I was doing and why. Finally I worked up enough nerve to say to him, "Brother Copeland, do you mind if I ask you some questions?"

"Not at all," he answered. "What do you want to know?"

"Well, the fact of the matter is that I have some real financial problems," I told him honestly, "and I don't know what to do about them. Now I have no trouble believing God for healing. I found that divine health is part of the atonement, so I accept it and walk in it. But how do you talk God into meeting your financial needs? What does a person have to do to get God to help him out with his finances?"

I will never forget Brother Copeland's answer: "God has already done all He is going to do about your finances."

"Are you kidding me?" I asked in shock. "You don't mean that He is going to leave me in this mess, do you?"

"No," he said. "I mean that He has already done all He is going to do about your finances, just as He has already done all He is going to do about your healing. He sent Jesus to the cross to bear your sickness and disease. You are able to accept that by faith. You don't have to have Jesus come down and have stripes laid on His back every time you need physical healing. He was made sick that you might have His health. In the same way, He was made poor that you might be made rich. So God has done everything that He is going to do in that area, just as in the area of salvation and healing."

"That's wonderful," I replied. "But how do I appropriate that?"

And he began to teach me. I started following his teaching, and it has worked for me ever since. It is that teaching that I am sharing with you in these pages so that you too will prosper just as I have been doing all these years since that informative and inspiring talk with Brother Copeland.

We see from the Word of God that the Lord has a system of finance. God has a plan for our material prosperity. But that plan will not be set in action automatically just because we are Christians. We have to appropriate the blessings of God.

In regard to finances, there are spiritual laws that must be followed and applied if we are to prosper. The first of these laws, as we have seen in Malachi 3, pertains to the tithe. No one can expect to be prospered and blessed by the Lord, to have so many blessings poured out upon him that he has to cry, "Stop, that's enough!" unless he is first obedient to the Lord by bringing in all the tithe.

But that is not the only spiritual law of finances. There are others throughout the Scriptures. That's one reason that regular Bible reading is so important in our daily lives.

Laws of Poverty

Yet a little sleep, a little slumber, a little folding of the hands to sleep:

So shall thy poverty come as one that travelleth, and thy want as an armed man.

Proverbs 6:10,11

The same Bible that gives us the laws of prosperity also gives us the laws that govern or create poverty. One of these laws is quoted above. It states, in essence, that all a person has to do to get into poverty is to take to his bed and not get up. In more formal terminology, the law is: poverty is the natural and unavoidable consequence of laziness.

Prosperity Is a Lifestyle ∨

There are laws that produce prosperity, and the wise person will choose those laws and walk in them. If there are laws, then there will be opposition, because all laws are going to be opposed. These laws will be opposed because they work. But they will not work automatically; they have to be applied prayerfully and diligently. Neither will they produce results overnight; they must become a lifestyle.

We must get out of the mindset of "trying" God's laws to see if they work. Because when the devil hears us say, "I am going to try it God's way," what he hears is a lack of commitment. He knows that all he has to do is to create a few barriers, throw up a few obstacles, and we will give up. That's what happens when we "try it God's way." The rule is: you can't try it; you've got to do it.

If you are married, what was your response when you were asked, "Do you take this person as your lawfully wedded husband/wife?" Did you answer, "Well, I'll try"? That is not the right answer. The correct response is, "I do." You can't try marriage. To do so is to guarantee failure. That's the reason so many marriages are falling apart today, because people are going into marriage with a "try it and see" attitude. That makes it too easy to decide that it doesn't work.

The same is true of the spiritual laws of prosperity. You cannot try them; you've got to do them. Even when it looks as if they are not working.

We have said that diet and exercise do no good unless they are adhered to carefully, consistently, continually, constantly, and conscientiously. No one can try to follow a diet or exercise program off and on for a while and expect any kind of positive, lasting results. Yet many Christians do precisely that when it comes to God's laws of prosperity. They tithe for a month or two, and when they don't see any instant results, they conclude that the law of tithing and blessing doesn't work. The problem is that they applied an *action* while God prescribed a *lifestyle.* There is a big difference between the two.

The laws of God work only when they are lived out day by day. When God's laws become a lifestyle instead of a try, they will produce triumph instead of trial. Simply stated: God's laws work. But they work only for those who have made up their mind to follow them come what may, whether they *seem* to work or not.

But they *do* work.

Properly Applied, God's Laws Work

I am reminded of what Brother Copeland's father once told him: "You know, Kenneth, if I woke up tomorrow morning and found out that God didn't exist, that Jesus never was, and that the Bible is not true, I'd go right on living this way, because *it works.*"

In the natural realm today, everything seems to be going against us. The economy is bad. There are scandals on every side. People don't know whether they should give to Christian missions or not. As a result, my ministry, along with many others, has been put to the test. But the Lord has given me a word which has revolutionized my life. I shared that word with my staff, put it into action, and it worked! As a result, our desperate financial situation has been completely turned around.

Since that time our continual, pressing financial problem has disappeared. We have the money coming in each month to meet our every need. Our huge deficit has been wiped out. All this is unheard of for an organization of our size and scope. It is unbelievable for us to be able to pay cash for everything we purchase or order. The reason we are able to do that now is because we never stopped giving even in the darkest depths of our need. When our deficit was the greatest, we dug the deepest. We followed one of the basic spiritual laws that I have been discussing in these pages: don't eat your seed. That is, when you are down to the bottom of the barrel, like the poor widow of Zarephath, don't eat that last vital measure of grain and oil, but instead use it as a seed-gift. (1 Kings 17:1-16.) The result will be as powerful and effective for you as it was for that poor widow, and as it was for us in our desperate situation.

Another of God's spiritual laws of prosperity is that if we will be faithful to give to meet the needs of others, He will meet our needs from His riches in glory by Christ Jesus. (Phil. 4:19.) Notice that it is not in accordance to the beggarly elements of this world that God provides for His own, but in accordance to His riches in glory.

If you are faithfully following and applying the spiritual laws of prosperity found in the pages of the Bible, God can and will meet your financial needs — regardless of what they may be. Whatever your situation, God can turn it around if you expect it, and if you appropriate the spiritual laws that He has set forth in His Word.

Now let's look at some examples of God's turning a financial crisis into a financial miracle.

8

Scriptural Accounts of Turned Captivity

There was a man in the land of Uz, whose name was Job; and that man was perfect and upright, and one that feared God, and eschewed evil.

And there were born unto him several sons and three daughters.

His substance also was seven thousand sheep, and three thousand camels, and five hundred yoke of oxen, and five hundred she asses, and a very great household; so that this man was the greatest of all the men of the east.

Job 1:1-3

How do you suppose Job was able to amass such a huge fortune? The answer is revealed to us in verse 1 which tells us that he was perfect and upright, that he feared God and eschewed or turned away from evil.

In Psalm 1:1-3 we read these words:

Blessed is the man that walketh not in the counsel of the ungodly, nor standeth in the way of sinners, nor sitteth in the seat of the scornful.

But his delight is in the law of the Lord; and in his law doth he meditate day and night.

And he shall be like a tree planted by the rivers of water, that bringeth forth his fruit in his season; his leaf also shall not wither; and whatsoever he doeth shall prosper.

When God chose Abraham to leave his father's house and his native land and to go where He would send him,

He promised him that if he would walk perfectly and uprightly before Him and hearken diligently unto the voice of His Word, then God would bless him and make him to be a blessing. (Gen. 12:1,2.) In the very next chapter, we see that God has already blessed Abraham so much that he is **...very rich in cattle, in silver, and in gold** (Gen. 13:2). In fact, Abraham was so blessed with goods that he and his nephew Lot had to go separate ways because there was not enough land to support them both due to their great possessions. (Gen. 13:5-12.)

Like Abraham, Job became a rich man because he honored God. Job feared the Lord and walked in uprightness before Him. As a result, God made him wealthy.

Satan's Test of Job

Now there was a day when the sons of God came to present themselves before the Lord, and Satan came also among them.

And the Lord said unto Satan, Whence comest thou? Then Satan answered the Lord, and said, From going to and fro in the earth, and from walking up and down in it.

And the Lord said unto Satan, Hast thou considered my servant Job, that there is none like him in the earth, a perfect and an upright man, one that feareth God, and escheweth evil?

Then Satan answered the Lord, and said, Doth Job fear God for nought?

Hast not thou made an hedge about him, and about his house, and about all that he hath on every side? thou hast blessed the work of his hands, and his substance is increased in the land.

But put forth thine hand now, and touch all that he hath, and he will curse thee to thy face.

And the Lord said unto Satan, Behold, all that he hath is in thy power; only upon himself put not forth

thine hand. So Satan went forth from the presence of the Lord.

Job 1:6-12

God's great blessing on Job and His boasting of him and his righteousness made Satan jealous and angry, so he challenged God to put Job to the test.

Satan said to God, "Why shouldn't Job serve and honor You? You have built a hedge of blessing and protection around him. If You will tear down that hedge, if You will lay Your hands on his possessions, he will curse You to Your face."

Notice that the Lord would not tear down the hedge around Job, nor would He set His hand against His devoted servant. To prove Job's character and integrity, however, He did tell Satan, "He is in your power; do to his precious possessions as you will. But you cannot lay a hand on Job himself."

What God was saying is this: "I know this man. No matter what you do to him, he will not turn his back on Me. He will not curse Me, nor even stop serving Me."

God was that sure of Job. He was like a trophy to the Lord.

So Satan went out of the presence of the Lord to begin his attacks upon Job. You know the story, how Satan set about to destroy Job's possessions, his children, and all that he owned. Yet verse 22 of this same chapter tells us: **In all this Job sinned not, nor charged God foolishly.**

Later on, in Chapter 2, we read that Satan again appeared before the Lord and received permission to strike Job himself with sickness and disease. Job's situation became so severe that his own wife said to him, **...Dost thou still retain thine integrity? curse God, and die** (Job 2:9). But even then Job refused to blame God for his over-whelming misfortunes.

According to most theologians, the time of Job's suffering probably lasted a full year. If that is so, then it had to be the worst year in any man's life. But at the same time it is encouraging. Why do I say that? Because we see that although Satan fired his best shots at Job, although he launched his heaviest artillery at him, although he threw everything in his vast arsenal against him, he could not make this faithful man turn his back on God. That tells me that if Job could endure that kind of punishment and pressure, which was far greater than anything most of us will ever have to face, then we can surely endure whatever the devil may bring against us.

Not only that, I am encouraged because in the New Testament the Apostle Paul states that with every trial, every test, every temptation that Satan brings against us, God will provide a way of escape so that we can see it through and emerge victorious from it. (1 Cor. 10:13.)

But the greatest encouragement I draw from this story of faithful Job is found at the very end, in the final chapter of the book.

All's Well That Ends Well!

And the Lord *turned the captivity of Job*...: and *the Lord gave Job twice as much as he had before.*
Job 42:10

Here we see again the unique ability that God has to turn a financial crisis into a financial miracle. If God could turn this man's tragedy into a triumph, surely He can do something about the circumstances you and I are facing at the moment.

I don't know of anyone who has been through what Job endured. Some of us may have experienced a few of the hardships, losses, and tragedies that befell Job. But I dare say that no one among us has had to endure all of them, and certainly not within a one-year period of time. If God could take Job's hopeless situation and turn it so that he ended up with twice as much as he had before, that is greatly encouraging to me — and it should be so to you. That is precisely what the story was given to us for.

The Power of Patience

Contrary to what you may have been led to believe, the Book of Job is not a sad story, a story of suffering and defeat. It is a happy story, a story of perseverance and victory, as we see in the writings of one of the New Testament disciples:

> Behold, *we count them happy which endure.* Ye have heard of the patience of Job, and *have seen the end of the Lord;* that the Lord is very pitiful, and of tender mercy.
> James 5:11

The *New International Version* of this verse reads: **As you know, *we consider blessed those who have persevered.* You have heard of Job's perseverance and *have seen what the Lord finally brought about.* The Lord is full of compassion and mercy.**

If you were to ask most Christians what the main theme of the Book of Job is, the majority of them would say trials and tests. But that is not what the Book of Job is all about. The crux of the Book of Job is patience.

Notice that James did not say, "You have heard of the trials and tests of Job." Instead, he says, "You have heard of the patience of Job."

What we should get out of reading the Book of Job is a lesson in what patience will produce. As we see in the *New International Version*, patience is perseverance; it is constancy, consistency, refusal to change in the face of outward circumstances. So when James says that we have heard of the patience of Job, he is saying that we should all be familiar with the perseverance, the tenacity, the stability, the determination, the staying power of Job.

Every time we read this book we ought to exclaim, "Dear God, look at the power of patience demonstrated here!"

What is the "power of patience"? James tells us about it in chapter 1, verses 2 through 4:

> **My brethren, count it all joy when ye fall into divers temptations;**
>
> **Knowing this, that the trying of your faith worketh patience.**
>
> **But let patience have her perfect work, that ye may be perfect and entire, wanting nothing.**

What James is telling us here is that if we will let patience have her perfect work in our life, if we will endure to the end, if we will remain constant even in the midst of adversity, if we will count it all joy, we will be perfect, entire, wanting nothing.

The *New International Version* of verse 4 reads: **Perseverance must finish its work so that you may be mature and complete, not lacking anything.**

According to James, if we will be patient, if we will allow patience to have her perfect work, if we will continue to persevere in spite of outward circumstances, we will lack nothing. That means that we will end up receiving what we have believed for all through the tests and trials and tribulations of life.

I realize that most Charismatics don't like that word *patience* any more than they like the word *discipline.* I understand why patience has a negative connotation to so many believers. I know what it is like to stand in faith and go on standing and standing and standing, only to be told by some preacher that the reason the answer has not manifested is because of a lack of patience. Frankly, sometimes that's enough to make me want to slap somebody's face and seek forgiveness later! I have even gone too far as to declare, "If another preacher tells me to be patient, I'm going to hit him. I don't care if God sees it or not. I've been patient long enough, and I'm tired of it."

In fact, according to the old joke, that is the way most of us pray: "Oh, Lord, give me patience — and give it to me right this minute!"

Obviously, that is not patience. Do you know what patience really is? A good definition of the word *patience* is found in the seventeenth verse of the first chapter of James in which he writes: **Every good gift and every perfect gift is from above, and cometh down from the Father of lights, with whom is** *no variableness, neither shadow of turning.*

That is patience as demonstrated by God Himself: no variableness, no changing, no shadow of turning. According to the Bible, God is patient. (Rom. 15:5.) He is longsuffering. (Num. 14:18.) He changes not. (Mal. 3:6.) He is the same yesterday, and today, and forever. (Heb. 13:8.) That is the way we must be if we are to withstand tests, trials, and temptations and end up lacking nothing.

God lives by faith. That is, He is not moved by what He sees, but by what He knows. If He were moved by what He sees, He would have given up on us long ago. Despite our weaknesses and failures, God goes right on believing in us, forgiving us, helping us, supporting us, and loving us. And in the end, He will see us through to final victory — if we will display the same kind of patience and perseverance and trust in Him that He shows in us.

Obviously, God knows something that we need to learn: the power of patience.

The Role of Patience in Turning Captivity

You may need a financial miracle, a financial turnaround in your life. If so, I can promise you that patience is going to play a very important role in that financial miracle. Why? Because that turnaround may not be manifest overnight.

It took eighteen months for our deficit to be wiped away. But who cares how long it took, as long as it happened? There are people in business who spend their entire lives working to get out from under a large debt.

Brother Kenneth Copeland tells how the Lord helped him and his ministry wipe out a $5.6 million deficit. I don't see that as a defeat but as a victory. I think it is nothing short of miraculous to be able to believe for and receive $5.6 million dollars — above and beyond the normal operating expenses of a worldwide ministry — and in a relatively short time.

What difference does it make how long it takes to erase your deficit, as long as you end up debt-free? The important thing is not time but results.

We in the Body of Christ have got to quit being so time-conscious. The devil will rob us of our victory if we keep trying to place restrictions on God. What we have got to determine is that we are going to be patient and see our situation through to victory regardless of how long it may take.

That's what James meant when he wrote that we consider those people blessed or happy who endure. That's just the opposite of the way most people view endurance. How many folks do you know who, when they are informed that they must endure, suddenly get all excited and break out into a bright, cheerful smile? Yet that is precisely what we are told to do in this passage — to count it all joy. That means that we should count it a privilege to endure. Why? Because we know that at the end of our time of endurance, there will be our time of triumph.

Through the first forty-one chapters of Job's trials and tribulations there is not much to make anyone rejoice. But at the end of the book, in the forty-second chapter, when

God turns Job's captivity and restores his fortunes twofold, then there is every reason for rejoicing.

What we ought to derive from our study of the Book of Job is not an appreciation of how much he had to suffer or how long he had to endure, but how miraculously and wonderfully God turned his captivity into triumph. We should come away with a revelation and a better understanding of what patience and perseverance will do in the life of a person who won't give up even in the worst adversity. God will turn that individual's crisis into victory.

The End of the Lord

James says that we have heard of the patience of Job and have seen **the end of the Lord** (James 5:11). What does he mean by that last expression? He means that we have seen what God does in the end for patient people.

What did James say the Lord is like? He is **very pitiful and of tender mercy,** or as the *New International Version* translates it, **full of compassion and mercy**.

In the story of Job we see the compassion and mercy of God motivate Him to intervene on behalf of those who practice patience and perseverance. God is not going to allow patient people to be defeated, to be overcome by the enemy, to be robbed of their victory. Instead, He will turn their captivity into triumph.

It would be wonderful if all we had to do is to say, "God, I have a need," and the Lord would spring forth and provide the solution to that crisis instantly. That would be marvelous. But you know as well as I that that sort of thing doesn't happen very often.

Thank God for instant results. I have had many in my own experience. But that is not the story of my life. Like most Christians, I live between the "amen" and the "there it is." I pray; I believe that I receive. I'm always on my way to "there it is." And by the time what I am praying and believing for is manifested, I am already involved in praying and believing for another "there it is."

It would be wonderful if our prayers worked instantaneously. But if that were the case, there would be nothing to build the character of Jesus in our lives.

Paul knew that things do not happen instantly all the time. That's what he meant when he spoke about **having done all, to stand** (Eph. 6:13).

"But, I've been standing for eighteen months."

Stand.

"How much longer?"

Stand.

"When will it all be over?"

Stand.

"Aren't you going to help me?"

Stand.

"Don't you feel sorry for me?"

Stand.

I know how you feel. I know from experience how it feels to have so many fiery darts in your shield of faith that you can't hold it up any longer. There have been times that I have felt as if my breastplate of righteousness was slipping and my helmet of salvation was toppling from my head, as if my belt of truth was falling down around my feet, my sword of the Spirit was dull, and my arm worn out with wielding it. I have been so fatigued from resisting that I have cried out to God, "Lord, I can't endure it any longer."

His answer has always been, "Yes, but you are still standing. So go on standing."

"But what do I do then, Lord?"

His answer was simple: "Rejoice."

"But why?"

"Because you have got the devil right where you want him."

"But how can that be?"

"If you knew what I know, you would understand. Satan has just fired his best shot. You are tired, even wobbling on your feet. But you are still standing. So rejoice; victory is in sight!"

If this is the way you feel right now, then rejoice and be exceeding glad. You are about to win! But in order to carry off the victory, you must be patient. You must be like Job.

Everyone has heard of the patience of Job. And everyone wants the results that Job received. But unfortunately most of us don't want to do what Job did to receive those results. What did Job do? He endured. He stood. He exercised perseverance. He was patient.

If you want a financial miracle today, then be assured that patience is going to play a vital role in that miracle.

The Creditor Is Coming

Now there cried a certain woman of the wives of the sons of the prophets unto Elisha, saying, Thy servant my husband is dead; and thou knowest that thy servant did fear the Lord: and the creditor is come to take unto him my two sons to be bondmen.

2 Kings 4:1

As we consider some other vital ingredients for turning a financial crisis into a financial miracle, let's examine the case of this poor widow. She definitely has a financial problem. The creditors are coming to take her sons as payment for her debts.

Now you may think that your situation is severe because you owe money to the finance company, the bank, the savings and loan, the mortgage holder or whomever. But is your situation so severe that your creditors are coming to take your children away from you? Did you sign away your firstborn as security for your loans? I dare say not. But that is exactly the case with this woman. I would definitely classify her situation as a financial crisis, wouldn't you?

She has no means, she thinks, to solve this pressing problem, and nowhere to turn for help. In the natural she has no resource at all, or so it would appear. But notice what happens when she appeals to the prophet for guidance and direction.

What Hast Thou?

And Elisha said unto her, What shall I do for thee? tell me, what hast thou in the house? And she said, Thine handmaid hath not any thing in the house, save a pot of oil.

Then he said, Go, borrow thee vessels abroad of all thy neighbours, even empty vessels; borrow not a few.

And when thou art come in, thou shalt shut the door upon thee and upon thy sons, and shalt pour out into all those vessels, and thou shalt set aside that which is full.

2 Kings 4:2-4

This passage is very important. We need to get hold of what it is saying to us in our situations. Many times we think, "How can God turn my situation around? I don't have anything for Him to work with. There is absolutely nothing I can do." But yet we always have *something*. Even in the worst of conditions or circumstances, there is always *something* that we can do.

You may think that God cannot bless your giving because you have nothing to give. This woman didn't think she had anything either; that's why she cried out in despair to the man of God. But even the poorest of us has something of value that God can multiply for a harvest of good to us and to others.

One time a man gave me the buttons off his shirt with a little note that read, "This is all I have. You'll have to believe for the shirt to go with them."

That's all that man had. But it was something.

I have preached in areas in the world where there was no money at all among the inhabitants. In Africa the people brought me a chicken as a love offering. That may seem insignificant except that you must realize that this was the only chicken in the village. It was all they had to give, the modern-day equivalent of the widow's two mites in Jesus' era. (Mark 12:41-44.)

One time while I was preaching out in the bush country of Kenya, East Africa, after the service the people brought me a goat. I thought, "How in the world am I going to get that thing home with me?" Actually, of course, I had no intention of trying to ship that animal all the way back to the United States. But I had to accept it graciously from the people because it meant so much to them — and to me. In fact, I was so touched by their act of love and generosity that I began to weep. I couldn't quit crying. Because I knew that was the only goat in that village and that it represented the total milk supply for the children of that area. It was the villagers' most prized possession. And they wanted to give their very best to the man of God. That is a humbling experience, I can assure you.

Yet you and I sit here in our mechanized, industrialized, affluent society surrounded by luxuries only dreamed about by the majority of the world's population and complain that we have nothing to give. Yes we do. We just haven't looked hard enough.

This woman didn't think she had anything to give either, until the prophet asked her, "What do you have in your house?"

"Well, I've got one little pot of oil," she said in essence.

And that "one little pot of oil" was all that God was looking for. Not because of its great value, but because of what it represented.

You see, in order to turn a financial crisis into a financial miracle, two things are necessary: number one is obedience, and number two is a point of contact, something that can be pointed to as a release or springboard for faith.

A Point of Contact

And a woman having an issue of blood twelve years, which had spent all her living upon physicians, neither could be healed of any,

Came behind him, and touched the border of his garment: and immediately her issue of blood stanched.

And Jesus said, Who touched me? When all denied, Peter and they that were with him said, Master, the multitude throng thee and press thee, and sayest thou, Who touched me?

And Jesus said, Somebody hath touched me: for I perceive that virtue is gone out of me.

And when the woman saw that she was not hid, she came trembling, and falling down before him, she declared unto him before all the people for what cause she had touched him, and how she was healed immediately.

And he said unto her, Daughter, be of good cheer: thy faith hath made thee whole; go in peace.

Luke 8:43-48

In the case of the woman with the issue of blood who came secretly behind Jesus seeking healing, the point of contact was the touch of His garment.

Scriptural Accounts of Turned Captivity

In Mark's account of this same event, we read that the woman said to herself, **...If I may touch but his clothes, I shall be whole** (Mark 5:28). And it happened just as she had said. Because she had established the point of contact that released her faith.

But notice what Jesus did when she sneaked up in the crowd and touched Him. He asked, "Who touched Me?" His disciples said to Him, "Master, You are surrounded and jostled on all sides. There are dozens of people touching You. What do You mean by asking, 'Who touched Me?' Everyone is touching You."

"No, this was different," He answered in essence. "This was a touch of faith. Because I felt healing virtue go out of Me."

"Somebody made a demand on My ability." That demand on the ability of Jesus is made by obedience and a point of contact.

The Key of Obedience

So she went from him, and shut the door upon her and upon her sons, who brought the vessels to her; and she poured out.

2 Kings 4:5

Notice that obedience was required of the widow in financial crisis because the prophet commanded her to borrow vessels from all of her neighbors, to shut herself and her sons in their house, and to begin pouring out the oil into the borrowed vessels as long as it lasted.

In the natural, it would seem that he was asking her to do something foolish. If you take a pot of oil and pour its contents into another pot, all you have done is transfer the same oil from one container to another. How was that supposed to help this poor woman pay her debts?

The widow could have protested to the prophet, "That's stupid. I'm not going to do that. It's a waste of time and effort. Why should I go around borrowing pots and pans from my neighbors just so I can pour out what little oil I have left into one of them. I don't need all those vessels. If I have a little dab of oil in one container, why do I need more containers? I won't do it."

What God tells us to do in order to turn our financial crisis into a financial miracle may seem foolish to us and to others. But no matter how foolish or illogical it may seem, we must do as we are told if we are to be blessed of the Lord because the key to the miraculous is obedience.

Despite how she may have felt, the widow did as she was told. That is a vitally important aspect of this story.

Do you remember the account of the first miracle that Jesus ever performed in Cana of Galilee? When the family ran out of wine to serve their guests, they came to Mary, the mother of Jesus, and told her about their embarrassing situation. Mary exercised faith by taking the initiative: **His mother saith unto the servants, Whatsoever he saith unto you, do it** (John 2:5).

And what Jesus said to them sounded foolish. He told them to fill up some huge jugs with water and then draw some out and take it to the master of ceremonies.

You and I know that pouring water into a jug and then drawing it back out does not alter the chemical composition of the water. But in this case there was an exception made to the natural order of things because by the time the master of ceremonies tasted the water from the jug, it had been *turned* into wine. (There's that word again!)

Here we see that obedience opens the door to the miraculous.

That was true for the poor widow in the Old Testament. It was true for the wine stewards in the New Testament. And it is true for us today.

Go, Sell,
Pay, and Live

And it came to pass, when the vessels were full, that she said unto her son, Bring me yet a vessel. And he said unto her, There is not a vessel more. And the oil stayed.

Then she came and told the man of God. And he said, Go, sell the oil, and pay thy debt, and live thou and thy children of the rest.

2 Kings 4:6,7

The reason this story is so up-to-date is because the people of that era were experiencing an oil shortage just as we are in some locations today. The good news is that obedience and a point of contact work just as well today as they did in the days of the Old and New Testaments.

This widow was obedient to the word of the Lord. As we have noted, her obedience was a vitally important aspect in receiving her miracle. The same is true of you and me today. Once we hear the word of God, we must not lean on the arm of flesh. This lesson was brought home to me in an unforgettable way over a decade ago.

In October 1981 while preaching in Brother Kenneth Copeland's Believer's Convention in Charlotte, North Carolina, I received a supernatural visitation from the Lord. I did not seek it or ask for it. I had never even imagined such a thing happening to me. The Lord simply appeared to me in my hotel room and began to speak to me about financial miracles. At that time, He told me something that I will never forget. He led me to the twenty-sixth chapter of Genesis in which is described a terrible famine that was ravaging the land. It brought to mind the kind of situation we are facing in our day.

I saw on the news just recently while ministering in Great Britain that the railway industry was laying off five thousand workers. Another three thousand were being let go somewhere else, and another five hundred in another place.

In the natural, things are not looking good. Businesses and industry are experiencing financial difficulties and are reducing costs and overhead wherever they can. Workers are being laid off. Jobs are being eliminated. The unemployment rate, although sometimes improving, has increased dramatically. Banks and savings and loan institutions are failing. Bankruptcies are rampant. Inflation is again on the rise. The national debt is skyrocketing out of control. Economic unrest and instability are having an adverse effect on every area of our lives both nationally and internationally.

Faced with that kind of depressing economic situation, you and I have no other choice but to get on God's system, because it is the only system that is working. That's why I urge people to get on it now and not to wait until the famine has struck with full force. Because if things look bad now, if you think that the world's system is failing at this point, you haven't seen anything yet. The entire system is crumbling. It is all falling apart. It is being torn down bit by bit. It will soon get to the place that no one can trust anything that man has built.

When that happens, only those who are on God's system will be able to stand head and shoulders above the crowd and say, "Our God supplies all our need according to His riches in glory by Christ Jesus."

So once you hear the word of God, don't lean on the arm of flesh.

This poor widow heard the word of God to her: "Go, borrow vessels and pour your remaining oil into them. Don't borrow just a few."

Notice that God is abundance-minded. God is not only interested in meeting our immediate need, He also wants

122

us to have enough left over to live off of for years to come. That's why He told this lady not to borrow just a few vessels.   √

She did as she was told, and as a result, she had enough oil to sell to pay off her debt and to live on the rest. That is the abundance of God. He will not only get us out of debt, but will turn our financial crisis into a financial victory. He will not only provide us enough to live on, but also enough to help somebody else out of their crisis.

That is what the Lord was revealing to me when He appeared to me in 1981 and began to teach me about how to prosper in the midst of famine. In these last crucial pages I would like to share with you what the Lord revealed to me in that visitation.

Go Not Down to Egypt

And there was a famine in the land, beside the first famine that was in the days of Abraham. And Isaac went unto Abimelech king of the Philistines unto Gerar.

And the Lord appeared unto him, and said, Go not down into Egypt; dwell in the land which I shall tell thee of;

Sojourn in this land, and I will be with thee, and will bless thee; for unto thee, and unto thy seed, I will give all these countries, and I will perform the oath which I sware unto Abraham thy father;

And I will make thy seed to multiply as the stars of heaven, and will give unto thy seed all these countries; and in thy seed shall all the nations of the earth be blessed;

Because that Abraham obeyed my voice, and kept my charge, my commandments, my statutes, and my laws.

Genesis 26:1-5

In the midst of famine the Lord appeared to Isaac and renewed the covenant with him that He had made with his father Abraham. Because of the faithfulness of Abraham, the Lord promised to bless Isaac abundantly and to make him to be a blessing to many others. Here again we see the long-term consequences of obedience.

The good news for us is that as Abraham's spiritual seed through Jesus Christ, all these blessings are ours as well. (Gal. 3:7-9,13,14.)

The Lord also instructed Isaac about what to do in the face of the famine. He commanded him not to go down to Egypt but to dwell in the land that He would show him, assuring him that he would do well there.

In the Old Testament, Egypt was always a symbol or shadow or type of "the arm of flesh." So what the Lord was telling Isaac was not to go the way of the world, because that system was failing, just as it is today. He was warning him not to look to the arm of the flesh, but to look to Him as his Source. The Lord promised Isaac that if he would be obedient, He would do for him as He had for his father Abraham, that he would bless him supernaturally.

The Lord was also warning Isaac not to try to run from his problems.

All these things that God told Isaac, the seed of Abraham, in Old Testament days, He is telling us, the seed of Abraham, today. We are not to look to the arm of flesh for our sustenance, but to the Lord. We are not to try to run away from our problems, but to stay and face them head on. We are not to try to escape from famine, but to learn to prosper in the midst of famine.

Sow in Famine

Then Isaac sowed in that land, and received the same year an hundredfold: and the Lord blessed him.

> And the man waxed great, and went forward, and grew until he became very great:
>
> For he had possessions of flocks and possessions of herds, and great store of servants: and the Philistines envied him.
>
> Genesis 26:12-14

Notice that Isaac sowed in famine.

Now any good farmer knows that you don't do that. You don't sow good seed into the ground when there is no chance that it will germinate and reproduce. In famine, there is no water to irrigate the field. And without water, there is no crop, no harvest, no multiplied return.

Yet God told Isaac to stay in the land and to sow in famine. Because he was obedient to the Lord, Isaac reaped a magnificent return and was blessed beyond measure. It was truly a miracle.

If you are in a financial crisis today, don't stop sowing. Don't stop giving just because the conditions necessary for planting and reaping look so unfavorable. That is how you overcome famine, by sowing seed in the very midst of it.

Remember the agricultural and spiritual law that we have already set forth: don't eat your seed. When in a famine, don't eat that last bit of seed, but sow it in hope and earnest expectation of a multiplied harvest. That's what Isaac did. The Bible says that Isaac sowed in time of famine and the Lord gave him a hundredfold return in the same year. He became so wealthy that the Philistines envied him.

That will happen to God's people today in the time of our famine. In these last days, God's people are going to rise up in the power of the Lord and are going to prosper when nobody else does. The Bible says that the wealth of the sinner is laid up for the just. (Prov. 13:22.) Eventually all that wealth will come into our hands, and the world will be envious of us. But that will only happen if we do as

Abraham and Isaac did and learn to appropriate the laws of God.

Obedience and a point of contact always work to turn a financial crisis into a financial miracle.

I Have Commanded the Ravens

And Elijah the Tishbite, who was of the inhabitants of Gilead, said unto Ahab, As the Lord God of Israel liveth, before whom I stand, there shall not be dew nor rain these years, but according to my word.

And the word of the Lord came unto him, saying,

Get thee hence, and turn thee eastward, and hide thyself by the brook Cherith, that is before Jordan.

And it shall be, that thou shalt drink of the brook; and I have commanded the ravens to feed thee there.

And he went and did according unto the word of the Lord: for he went and dwelt by the brook Cherith, that is before Jordan.

And the ravens brought him bread and flesh in the morning, and bread and flesh in the evening; and he drank of the brook.

1 Kings 17:1-6

Do you realize that if people won't listen, God can speak to the birds of the air and command them to feed you?

Every time a bird flies over my house, I ask, "Is he the one, Lord?"

Every time an old dog comes by and starts to dig up my yard, "I say, 'Go to it, boy; dig, dig, dig.'"

Carolyn screams, "Get that mutt out of there, he's digging up my flowers." But I answer, "Leave him alone. God said that the hidden riches belong to me. That old dog may come up with some of them."

Every time I go fishing and reel in a catch, I open the fish's mouth and look inside to see if there is any tax money in there. I don't want to take any chances on missing out on God's miracle provision.

Now you may be thinking, "Jerry Savelle, you are a nut!"

I may be, but I am a happy, healthy, successful, prosperous nut. I believe that is because I do as the men and women of the Bible and put my faith and trust in the Lord and not in man.

Notice that when the king refused to listen to the prophet Elijah, the Lord intervened to rescue him from the famine that He had just pronounced upon the land. He sent Elijah to live by the brook Cherith where He commanded the birds of the air to bring him food twice a day.

I believe that the Lord will do the same for you and me if we will be obedient to His will and way for us. That kind of material provision is as much a part of the heritage of the saints of the Lord as salvation of our souls and divine health for our physical bodies. (Is. 54:17.)

I Have Commanded a Widow

And it came to pass after a while, that the brook dried up, because there had been no rain in the land.

And the word of the Lord came unto him, saying,

Arise, get thee to Zarephath, which belongeth to Zidon, and dwell there: behold, I have commanded a widow woman there to sustain thee.

1 Kings 17:7-9

I would like for you to notice something very important in this final passage we will examine from the Word of God. Even though the brook dried up in the place where God had sent Elijah, the Lord was already a step ahead of this event. He had already commanded a widow in Zarephath to take care of His servant.

God is always a step ahead of any event that may arise in our life. He is always ahead of a bad economy, a step ahead of unemployment, a step ahead of famine, a step ahead of inflation, a step ahead of recession, a step ahead of depression.

God is a step ahead of anything that may come our way. If we will just put our faith and trust in Him, if we will be obedient to His word for us, He will command His blessing upon us and cause us to prosper regardless of our situation or circumstances. He will turn all of our crises into triumphs. That too is the heritage of the saints of the Lord.

Dr. Jerry Savelle is a noted author, evangelist, and teacher who travels extensively throughout the United States, Canada, and overseas. He is president of Jerry Savelle Ministries, a ministry of many outreaches devoted to meeting the needs of believers all over the world.

Well-known for his balanced biblical teaching, Dr. Savelle has conducted seminars, crusades and conventions for more than twenty years as well as holding meetings in local churches and fellowships. He is being used to help bridge the gap between the traveling ministry and the local church. In these meetings, he is able to encourage and assist pastors in perfecting the saints for the work of the ministry. He is in great demand today because of his inspiring message of victory and faith and his accurate and entertaining illustrations from the Bible. He teaches the uncompromising Word of God with a power and an authority that is exciting, but with a love that delivers the message directly to the spirit man.

When Dr. Savelle was twelve years old, God spoke to his heart as he was watching the healing ministry of Oral Roberts on television. God told him that He was calling him into the ministry. Some years later, Dr. Savelle made Jesus Christ the Lord of his life, and since that time has been moving in the light of that calling.

Dr. Savelle is the founder of Overcoming Faith Churches of Kenya, and the mission outreach of his ministry extends to over more than fifty different countries around the world. His ministry also delivers the powerful message of God's Word across the United States through the JSM Prison Ministry Outreach.

Dr. Savelle has authored a number of books and has an extensive cassette teaching tape ministry. Thousands of books, tapes, and videos are distributed around the world each year through Jerry Savelle Ministries.

Other Books by Dr. Jerry Savelle

Faith Building Daily Devotionals
The Force of Joy
If Satan Can't Steal Your Joy, He Can't Keep Your Goods
Victory and Success Are Yours!
Sharing Jesus Effectively
Don't Let Go of Your Dreams
God's Provision for Healing
Purged by Fire
Right Mental Attitude
The Nature of Faith
The Established Heart

**Additional copies of this book are available
from your local bookstore.**

To contact the author, write:
Jerry Savelle Ministries
P. O. Box 748
Crowley, TX 76036

*Please include your prayer requests
and comments when you write.*

In Canada contact: Word Alive • P. O. Box 670
Niverville, Manitoba • CANADA ROA 1EO